THE NEW ORLEANS ITALIAN COOKBOOK

Italian-American Society of Jefferson Auxiliary

A FIREBIRD PRESS BOOK

PELICAN PUBLISHING COMPANY

Gretna 1998

First printing, November 1979
Second printing, November 1984
Third printing, March 1990

Library of Congress Cataloging in Publication Data

Italian-American heritage cook book of Jefferson.
The New Orleans Italian cookbook.

Reprint. Originally published: Italian-American
heritage cook book of Jefferson. Westwego, La. : Italian-
American Society of Jefferson Auxiliary, 1979.
Includes index.
1. Cookery, Italian. 2. Cookery—Louisiana—
New Orleans. 3. New Orleans (La.)—Social life and
customs. I. Italian-American Society of Jefferson.
Auxiliary. II. Title.
TX723.I78   1984   641.5945   84-20577
ISBN 1-56554-671-7

Manufactured in the United States of America

Published by Pelican Publishing Company, Inc.
1000 Burmaster Street, Gretna, Louisiana 70053

Table of Contents

Antipasto

ITALIAN OLIVE RELISH

1 quart, 32 ounce jar broken green olives
1 cup celery, cut in ¼ inch to ½ inch pieces
1 medium onion, chopped
1 carrot, cut in ¼ inch pieces
4 to 6 cloves garlic, minced
2 tablespoons capers, drained

2 teaspoons oregano
1 lemon juice; cut rind of half lemon in small pieces
¼ cup olive oil
¼ cup white vinegar
black pepper to taste

Drain and wash broken olives thoroughly; this is very important. Clean and reserve jar. Cut large olives in 8 pieces; small olives cut in 4 pieces.

In a large mixing bowl, add all ingredients and mix thoroughly. Marinate over night before serving. Return to cleaned olive jar and place remaining olive relish in any clean jar; never store in plastic container. If family members permit, Italian Olive Relish will remain in refrigerator in tightly sealed glass jar for 2 to 3 months. Always serve at room temperature.

Appetizer: Italian Olive Relish with crackers or Italian bread.

Salads: Italian Olive Relish in mixed green, crab, or combination salads. Use relish sparingly in potatoe or egg salads.

Sandwiches: Italian Olive Relish on hamburger, ham, combination or muffuletta sandwiches.

Seafood: Add ½ cup Italian Olive Relish to six marinated crabs; especially good.

Pizza: Add Italian Olive Relish and make a "party pizza" out of a peperoni, sausage, cheese or any plain pizza.

Marie Gattuso

1

SWEET AND SOUR OLIVES

INGREDIENTS:

2 tablespoons sugar
½ cup water
½ cup vinegar

1 pound black olives
1 pound onions
¼ cup olive oil

PROCEDURE:

Saute' onions in olive oil until light brown. Add drained olives and simmer for 5 minutes. Add vinegar and water and bring to a boil. Reduce heat and simmer 10 minutes until liquid thickens.

Katie Ceravolo

Caponiatina alla Sicilana

4 medium eggplants
1½ cups olive oil
4 onions, thinly sliced
2 cups diced celery
1 large can tomatoes
½ cup capers

1 tablespoon pine nuts
12 pitted, coarsely chopped
  black olives
½ cup sugar
½ teaspoon pepper

Peel and dice eggplants. Soak for 15 minutes in salted cold water. Drain dry on paper towels. Saute in one cup of oil until lightly browned. Remove eggplants from frying pan to sauce pan. Add remaining oil and onion.

Saute onions until soft and golden. Run tomatoes through a strainer and add to onion along with the celery.

Let simmer for about 15 minutes or so, add capers, olives, pine nuts and eggplants.
Heat vinegar in sauce pan. Dissolve sugar in vinegar and pour over eggplants. Add salt and pepper.

Adjust to taste and simmer 5 minutes, stirring frequently. Cool caponiatina before serving. The remainder may be stored in refrigerator.

Grace Panepinto

ANTIPASTO

INGREDIENTS:

1 cup olive oil
2 or 3 toes garlic
cooking oil
¼ pound green beans
small mushrooms
12 small onions, quartered
2 small green peppers, trimmed
  and cut in thin strips

1 stalk celery, cut up
1 bay leaf
12 large ripe olives
8 large green olives
3 slices pimento in small strips
1 cup ketchup
¼ cup wine vinegar
2 tablespoons sugar

2

2 carrots in small chunks
1 can eggplant appetizer

1 tablespoon mustard
salt and pepper to taste

PROCEDURE:

In a large saucepan, heat olive oil, garlic, and cook until it's golden. Discard garlic. Into hot oil, put green beans, mushrooms, onions, green peppers, carrots, eggplant appetizer, celery and bay leaf. Cook vegetables until tender. Stir in ripe olives, green olives, pimento, ketchup and wine vinegar, sugar, mustard, and salt and pepper. Cook 5 minutes longer. Store in refrigerator.

Mary Eason

CAPONATA
Cold Eggplant Appetizer

Makes Approximately 8 cups

2 pounds eggplant, peeled and cut in ½ inch cubes
(Approximately 4 small eggplants) Small eggplants because they are tender
½ cup olive oil
2 cups finely chopped celery
3/4 cup finely chopped onions
1/3 cup wine vineger mixed with
**   4 teaspoons sugar**
3 cups drained canned Italian plum tomatoes
2 tablespoons tomato paste
6 large green olives, pitted, slivered and well-rinsed
2 tablespoons capers
4 flat anchovy fillets, well rinsed and pounded smooth
**   (Be sure pounded to paste)**
Freshly ground black pepper

Sprinkle the cubes of eggplant generously with salt and set in a colander to drain over paper towels. After approximately 30 minutes, pat cubes dry with fresh paper towels and set aside. In heavy skillet, heat ¼ cup olive oil then add celery and cook over moderate heat stirring frequently for approximately 10 minutes. Then stir in the onions and cook for another 10 minutes or until celery and onions are soft and lightly colored. With a slotted spoon, transfer them to a bowl Pour the remaining ¼ cup olive oil in skillet and over high heat saute' the eggplant cubes stirring and turning them constantly approximately 8 minutes or until lightly browned. Return the celery and onions to skillet and stir in vinegar and sugar mixture, drained tomatoes, tomato paste, green olives, capers, anchovies, 2 teaspoons salt and a few grinds of pepper. Bring to a boil, reduce heat and simmer un-covered, stirring frequently for approximately 15 minutes. At this point, taste and season with salt and pepper and a little extra vinegar if necessary. Transfer to a serving bowl and refrigerate until ready to serve. Makes approximately 8 cups.

Sue Dandry

ANTIPASTO SARDI SALATI

INGREDIENTS:

12 sardi salati
Italian cheese, cubed
Black Italian olives
Italian bread

1 lemon
olive oil
black pepper

PROCEDURE:

Wash and fillet sardi (very easy to do). Sprinkle olive oil, lemon juice over sardis. Add pepper to taste. Arrange on tray along with Italian cheese, olives and bread.

Frank Vincent Zaccaria, Sr.

MARINATED MUSHROOMS

INGREDIENTS:

2/3 cup olive oil
1/3 cup wine vinegar
1 tablespoon worcestershire sauce
¼ teaspoon tabasco
1 teaspoon salt

pepper
1 tablespoon lemon juice
8 toes crushed garlic
2 7-8 ounce cans water-packed mushrooms (buttons)

PROCEDURE:

Mix first eight ingredients. Drain mushrooms well. Combine mushrooms and sauce and let stand at room temperature overnight. Serve as an appetizer.

Mrs. Esther Stringer

MARINATED FAVA BEANS

INGREDIENTS:

2 cups fava beans (leave bean with outer skin after removing from pod)
½ cup olive oil
1/3 cup rice vinegar
salt

black pepper
2 teaspoons cayenne pepper
6 toes mashed garlic

4

PROCEDURE:

Cook fava beans until tender. Drain. In lidded jar, mix next six ingredients. Add fava beans and marinate several days, stirring now and then. Serve using toothpicks. Can be added to tossed green salad.

Mrs. Dolores Zaccaria

"MOCK" ARTICHOKE DIP

INGREDIENTS:

1 16-ounce can french style string beans keeping liquid
1 cup Italian bread crumbs
1 cup parmesan cheese   5 toes garlic finely chopped
¼ cup olive oil   salt and pepper to taste

PROCEDURE:

Mix all above ingredients together. Heat at 375 degrees for 20 to 25 minutes until hot. Serve as a dip with party crackers.

ARTICHOKE SQUARES

INGREDIENTS:

1 can artichoke hearts   ½ cup oil
1 cup Italian bread crumbs   1 egg
½ cup Italian cheese   garlic (to taste)

PROCEDURE:

Preheat oven to 350 degrees. Drain hearts and set water aside in bowl. Mash hearts and add bread crumbs, cheese, garlic and oil. Add egg to water and beat. Add this to mixture and stir until well blended. Pour into a buttered casserole dish or pan, bake in 350 degree oven for 30 minutes. Let cool, refrigerate, cut into squares.

Constance Savoie

ARTICHOKE BALLS

INGREDIENTS:

2 cans artichoke hearts, drained (do not use marinated hearts)
1½ cups Italian style bread crumbs
1 cup Italian style bread crumbs (use to roll balls in)
1½ medium onions, chopped fine
4 toes garlic (use a press)
1½ - 2 cups fresh grated Romano cheese

2 tablespoons olive oil
salt and pepper to taste

PROCEDURE:

Mash artichoke hearts with a fork. Fry the onions slowly in the olive oil. Cook till onions become clear. Add all remaining ingredients except the 1 cup crumbs; cook for a few minutes to melt cheese. When mixture cools, roll into bite size balls. Use an ice tea spoon to scoop mixture for uniform size. Roll the balls in the one cup crumbs. Before serving, heat in a 300 degree oven 15-20 minutes. These can be served cold also. This can be kept frozen for at least 2 months.

This recipe can be adapted to a casserole by adding ½ - 1 cup water and put in a medium sized casserole. Sprinkle the top with several tablespoons of crumbs instead of 1 cup. Heat in a 350 degree oven for 25 minutes.

Linda Armbruster

ITALIAN FRIED ARTICHOKES

INGREDIENTS:

1 can 14 ounce quartered artichoke hearts
1 cup Italian bread crumbs
¼ cup grated Italian cheese
1 egg
½ cup milk
salt
pepper
garlic powder to taste

PROCEDURE:

Drain artichokes. Dip artichokes in egg and milk mixture. Mix bread crumbs and cheese and roll artichokes until coated. Deep fry until golden brown. String beans, cauliflower, eggplant can be used.

Gwen Ann DeLatte

ZUCCHINI APPETIZER

INGREDIENTS:

raw zucchini, sliced in thin strips and chilled
1 cup mayonnaise
1½ teaspoons curry powder
1 small grated onion
1 tablespoon lemon juice
2 crushed garlic pods

PROCEDURE:

Chill thin strips of zucchini. Mix the rest of the ingredients for the dip and chill. Serve cold.

Mrs. Mary Eason

FONDUTA
(Hot Melted Cheese with Toast)

INGREDIENTS:

3/4 pound Fontina cheese
1 cup milk
3 eggs beaten

salt and pepper
2 table spoons butter

PROCEDURE:

Dice the cheese. Cover with milk and let soak for a few hours. Add beaten eggs, salt, pepper and butter. Cook in double boiler -- stirring constantly. When the cheese melts and mixture turns creamy and smooth, pour into an earthenware bowl and serve with triangles of hot toast. The Fonduta may be garnished with thinly sliced raw mushrooms.

Grace Panepinto

SPITINI

INGREDIENTS:

2 cups Italian bread crumbs
1½ cups grated Romano or Parmesan Italian cheese
1½ blocks of butter or margarine, sliced thin
2 eggs   1 large round steak   salt
1 lemon   bay leaf   pepper

PROCEDURE:

Mix 1½ cups Italian bread crumbs and 1 cup of Italian cheese together, set aside. Beat eggs well, add salt and pepper to taste, set aside. Trim off any fat from meat and pound with meat pounder. Cut into squares 3 to 4 inches. Dip each piece one at a time in egg mixture, then bread mixture. On each square add ¼ teaspoon bread crumbs and cheese, ½ bay leaf, ½ thin slice of lemon and 1 thin slice of butter, fold over and close with toothpick. Place another thin slice of butter on top of each piece. Place in buttered shallow pan and bake at 350 degrees for 30 to 40 minutes or until done.

Rita Mae Martin

HAM AND MELON

INGREDIENTS:

Cantaloupe or honey dew melon (fully ripened)
Parma ham or boiled ham (sliced paper thin)

PROCEDURE:

Peel and slice melon. Drape 2 slices of ham over each melon slice.

Variation: Wrap ham slices around melon balls.

SPINACH-CHEESE ROLL-UPS

INGREDIENTS:

1 10-ounce frozen chopped spinach
1 carton Ricotta cheese (11 ounces)

1 3-ounce cream cheese
1 pound Mortadella or salami

PROCEDURE:

Cook spinach as directed. Drain and cool. Add cheeses to spinach. Mix well. Spread this mixture on slice of Mortadella and roll up jelly-roll fashion. Chill and serve.

Dolores Zaccaria

KATIE'S SPINACH BREAD

INGREDIENTS:

½ pound ham or fried crumbled bacon
½ cup olive oil
2 onions (chopped)
3 hard boiled eggs (chopped)
½ pound fresh spinach
½ pound yellow cheese (shredded)
½ pound Mozzarella cheese (shredded)

1 can whole tomatoes (in pieces)
1 can chopped black olives
salt and pepper to taste
1 pound bread dough

PROCEDURE:

Saute' onions in olive oil. Spread one half of dough on baking pan. (Use lard to spread dough.) Sprinkle all of the above ingredients over dough. Roll out top crust and cover the entire bottom layer. Bake until bread is done in 350 degrees.

Katie Ceravolo

SPINACH BREAD

INGREDIENTS:

1 box chopped frozen spinach (cook as directed)
½ pound Mozzarella cheese (diced)
½ cup olive oil
1 toe garlic (mashed)
salt and pepper to taste
dash sugar
1 can (2 ounces) flat fillets of chopped anchovies
1 pound bread dough
1 egg white
¼ cup Italian cheese (grated)

PROCEDURE:

Cook spinach as directed. Drain. Warm olive oil in sauce pan. Smash garlic toe; add to olive oil and saute' until garlic toe is golden brown. Remove garlic toe. Add spinach and mix well. Let cool. Add cheeses, seasonings and anchovies. Mix until well blended. Shape dough into two small French loaves. Spread open dough and place mixture in the center of each loaf. Fold bread around mixture. Use egg white to seal. Bake until bread is done. 350 degree oven. Serve hot.

Mrs. Dolores Zaccaria

MAMA'S SPINACH BREAD

INGREDIENTS:

1 16-ounce can spinach (chopped) or
1 pack of chopped frozen spinach (uncooked)
1 can fillet of anchovies (cut small)
½ cup of Italian cheese (cubed)
4 toes garlic or to taste
½ cup olive oil
Salt and Pepper to taste
1 pound of bread dough (homemade or bakery)

PROCEDURE:

Combine all ingredients (except dough). Marinate 2 hours or more. Divide dough into two parts. Roll flat into shape of bread loaf, spread half of filling in center of loaf. Fold and shape into loaf. Seal with egg white or olive oil. Bake in 350 degree oven until bread is golden brown.

Anna Mae Saluto St. Pierre

CREOLE - ITALIAN MUFFULETTA

INGREDIENTS:

Provolone cheese	olive salad
Genoa salami	muffuletta loaf with sesame seeds
Italian ham	

PROCEDURE:

Combine slices of cheese, salami, and ham with olive salad on muffuletta loaf bread -- a 10-inch crusty disc sprinkled with sesame seeds -- form a sandwich to feed two adults.

Frank Tusa
Central Grocery

PIZZA

BASIC DOUGH:

1 cake compressed yeast	1 teaspoon salt
1 cup lukewarm water	2 tablespoons olive oil
4 cups flour	

Dissolve yeast in water. Make well of flour, salt and yeast mixture. Knead for about 10 minutes. Add oil and knead until smooth. Place in a bowl, cover with wax paper and towel. Set in warm place. Let rise for about 2 hours. Spread dough in well greased baking pan about 15 inches by 11 inches and 3 inches deep.

FILLING:

¼ cup olive oil	½ pound mild Italian sausage
1 clove garlic	½ pound Mozzarella, sliced thin
½ minced onion	½ teaspoon oregano
2 cups tomatoes, canned	⅓ cup grated Romano cheese
salt and pepper	

Saute garlic and onion in oil. Remove garlic and add tomatoes and salt and pepper. Cook over medium heat about 20 minutes, crushing tomatoes with a slotted spoon. Meanwhile, cut sausage in ½ inch pieces and fry until brown in skillet. Remove. Cover dough with tomato sauce. Arrange sausage pieces and Mozzarella slices on top. Let rise for 10 minutes. Bake at 400 degrees for about 25 minutes or until golden brown. Serves 4.

Grace Panepinto

KING'S HOME MADE TAMALES

INGREDIENTS:

Number 1

2 pounds ground beef	½ teaspoon black pepper
1 pound ground pork	1 teaspoon oregano
5 teaspoons salt	1 cup white corn meal
3 teaspoons onion flakes	1 can 1½-ounce chili powder
2 teaspoons red pepper	1 cup cooking oil
2 teaspoons garlic powder	1 can 6-ounce tomato sauce

Number 2

1 can 6 ounce tomato paste	1 can 16-ounce chili tomatoes
1 can 6 ounce tomato sauce	1 can 1½-ounce chili powder

PROCEDURE:

Combine all ingredients of mix number 1 in a large deep pan and mix well. Pour a cup of white corn meal on table top. Shape meat mixture number 1 in medium size meatballs and roll in oblong shape. Wrap in tamale papers or shucks. Place them back in deep pan (turkey roaster).

Combine mixture number 2 in pitcher of hot water and mix well. Pour over pieced tamales and COMPLETELY cover with liquid. bring to a boil then simmer one hour. Makes approximately 72 tamales.

Voris King

Soups

GASTON SOUP

INGREDIENTS:

1 pound navy beans
1 pound pickel meat
1 onion (chopped)
2 ribs green onions

1 small head cabbage (cut in small sections)
3 potatoes (cut in four)
2 tablespoons parsley
salt and pepper to taste

PROCEDURE:

Boil beans on slow fire. Cut meat in cubes and boil about 10 minutes. Drain. Saute' onions. Add meat and seasoning to beans. Add cabbage one hour before beans are done. Add potatoes ½ hour before beans are done. Cook until creamy.

Clara Lucia Dubos

CHICKEN SOUP WITH SPINACH

INGREDIENTS:

3 chicken breasts
2 medium onions (chopped)
2 ribs celery (chopped)
1 small ripe tomato
   (peeled and chopped)
1 toe garlic (mashed)
salt and pepper to taste

spinach leaves
Provolone cheese (small pieces)
handful egg noodles
olive oil
parsley
Parmesan cheese (grated)

PROCEDURE:

In large pot, saute' onions, celery, tomato and garlic in two tablespoons olive oil. Add 1 quart water with chicken; season to taste.

12

Simmer until chicken is done. Remove chicken and debone. Cut in bite-size bits. Return to pot.

Wash and chop fresh spinach (about 10 leaves). Add spinach, cheese, noodles, and parsley to soup and simmer 10 minutes. Sprinkle with Parmesan cheese before serving.

Mrs. Dolores Zaccaria

LENTIL SOUP

INGREDIENTS:

1 pound bag lentils
2½ quarts cold water
1½ tablespoons salt
3 or 4 dashes chopped red pepper (if desired)
1 large onion (minced)
½ teaspoon dried thyme
1 cup diced ham (diced small)
1 tablespoon chopped parsley
3 or 4 pods of garlic (minced)
½ cup olive oil (or cooking oil)
2 bay leaf
3 or 4 carrots diced small
1 16-ounce can peeled Italian tomatoes and liquid

PROCEDURE:

Empty bag of lentils into collander - pick over lentils discarding bad pieces. Wash well. In large soup pot, combine lentils, 2½ quarts of water, salt and pepper. Bring to a boil, cover, reduce heat. Cook 1 hour.

Add all other ingredients, bring to boil, cover, reduce heat, cook 1 to 1½ hours. (Until lentils are very tender.) Adjust salt and pepper to taste. Serve piping hot --- Sprinkle with Parmesan cheese on top of each serving. Makes 8 servings.

Mrs. Nestor L. Currault, Jr.

JO-LO-LO OYSTER SOUP

INGREDIENTS:

1 stalk celery (chopped fine)
2 medium onions (chopped fine)
1 bunch green onions (chopped fine)
    separate bottoms from tops
1 pint water

1 pint oyster water
olive oil
2 tablespoons chopped parsley
6 dozen oysters

PROCEDURE:

In large pot, saute' celery, onions, green onions in olive oil. Add oysters, oyster water, water, 2 ounces white wine, hot sauce (to taste), and salt and pepper (to taste). Simmer ½ hour. Add parsley and onion tops and simmer 10 minutes.

Nat Chighizola

PASTA

Of all the foods which Italy has made her own, surely none is more widely associated with her than pasta. The Italian American without his spaghetti and meatballs is as mind-boggling a conception as the Roman without his fettuccine. It is a universally accepted fact that all Italians love pasta, and if they don't, they should, for properly prepared, a pasta dish can be truly epicurean.

The first decision the pasta cook must face is "homemade" or "store-bought". The latter is, of course, the easier method, but, as with most things in life, the easier road is not necessarily the better one. Fresh homemade pasta is light and delicate. It is I think, worth the extra or, at least, it's worth the extra effort or, at least, it's worth one try. The ingredients for six are 3½ cups all purpose unbleached flour or semolina, 5 eggs, and ¼ teaspoon salt. Very simply, first you mix everything (classically by breaking the eggs into the sunken center of the flour and salt mound and then slowly beating the mixture together), then you knead thoroughly the dough ball you have formed, roll it out very, very thinly on a floured surface, and finally cut it into the desired shapes.

Now all that is left is to cook it, but how indeed to cook it? The possibilities are endless. One can serve any number of different pastas with any number of different sauces: fettuccine, spaghetti, rigatoni, ziti, tonnarelli, macaroni, linguine or vermicelli with butter sauces, cream sauces, tomato sauces, or meat sauces, to name a few. Or one can stuff the pasta with meat, cheese, vegetables, whatever, to produce lasagne, cannelloni, ravioli,

15

manicotti, cappelletti or tortellini, to name a few. Or one can even add a little pasta to various broths to make hearty pots of soup.

If the cook is not now thoroughly confused, he or she is, alas, faced with one last decision. shall the pasta be served as a main course "alla Americana" or shall one do as the Romans do and present the pasta as a **primo piatto** (first course)? Homemade pasta is surely light enough to be followed by other courses, but the choice is certainly a personal one. Whatever you decide, pasta is fun, fun to cook and even more fun to eat.

Virginia Amato

PASTA

PASTA FOR SOUP

1. Conchigliette
2. Anellini
3. Nocchette
4. Acini di pepe
5. Semini di Melo

PASTA TO BE BOILED

12. Tagliatelle
13. Tagliatelle Verde
14. Fusilli
15. Capellini
16. Fedelini
17. Spaghetti
18. Spaghettini
19. Ziti
20. Mezzani
21. Perciatelli
22. Perciatelloni
23. Lasagnette
24. Lingue di Passero
25. Malfadine
26. Mafalde
27. Zitoni

PASTA TO BE STUFFED

6. Lumache
7. Agnolotti
8. Manicotti
9. Cannelloni
10. Ravioli
11. Tortellini

PASTA FOR BAKING

28. Lasagne
29. Curly Lasagne
30. Lasagne Verde
31. Occhi di Lupo
32. Conchiglie
33. Penne
34. Grosso Rigato
35. Pennini
36. Cappelletti
37. Spiedini
38. Elbow Macaroni
39. Ruote
40. Gramigna Rigata
41. Farfalle
42. Tortiglioni

PASTA AND BROCCOLI

INGREDIENTS:

1 bunch broccoli
1 pound pasta
½ cup olive oil
1 small onion, sliced fine

grated Parmesan cheese
1 clove garlic, minced
1 teaspoon basil
2 tablespoons chopped parsley

PROCEDURE:

Bring four quarts of water to boil in large pot. Salt the water and add broccoli which has been washed, pieced and broken up. Bring to a boil and cook 5 minutes. Add the paste to broccoli. Bring to a boil and cook until it's all done. Meanwhile, saute' onion, garlic, herbs in olive oil in skillet until the onions turn yellow. Drain the pasta and broccoli, reserving 1 cup of liquid. Mix pasta, broccoli, olive oil and onion mixture in large bowl. Add a little of the reserved liquid if desired. Serve with grated Parmesan cheese. Serves 6 persons.

Grace Panepinto

FAVE BEANS & PASTA (Macaroni)

INGREDIENTS:

1 large can fave beans
1 large onion
4 cloves garlic

6 tablespoons olive oil
salt and pepper to taste

PROCEDURE:

Skin fave beans and save liquid -- saute onions and garlic with olive oil, then put in liquid from fave beans. Cook down for approximately 10 minutes. Put fave beans in pot with sauted ingredients. Add 1 cup of water and simmer for 15 minutes. Boil macaroni separate. After fave is cooked, add Italian cheese to your taste and serve over macaroni.

Anna Mae St. Pierre

PASTA CARBONARA

INGREDIENTS:

2 small onions, chopped
2 tablespoons olive oil
2 tablespoons butter
½ cup dry white wine
5 slices bacon or prociutto, chopped

1 12-ounce bag spaghetti
3 eggs
chopped parsley
½ cup Romano cheese
sliced black olives or mushrooms
ground black pepper

PROCEDURE:

In a saucepan saute onions, with olive oil, butter, wine, bacon or prociutto. Cook together until wine evaporates. In a bowl, beat eggs with parsley, Romano cheese and black olives or mushrooms. Cook spaghetti al dente. Drain and put into bowl with egg mixture. Toss with onion mixture. Season with ground black pepper before serving.

Gloria Cristina

LASAGNE

MEAT SAUCE WITH TOMATOES:

Few drops cooking oil
1 small onion, chopped
1½ pounds ground lean meat (put salt and pepper while frying)
1 can pear shaped tomatoes or 1 large can tomato sauce
1 can tomato puree or 1 small can tomato paste
water if necessary, for sauce should be THICK
Sprinkle of oregano and sweet basil
¼ teaspoon garlic powder or puree
Sprinkle of parsley
2 ribs celery, chopped
3 or 4 small carrots, boiled and chopped
1 heaping tablespoon sugar
Salt and pepper to taste

PROCEDURE:

In large fry pan, heat cooking oil; add onion and ground beef, saute' until brown, stirring occasionally. Add garlic and parsley. Cook over low heat for 10 minutes. Add tomatoes and tomato puree, little water if necessary, oregano, sweet basil and sugar. Bring to boiling point and add celery, carrots, salt and pepper. Cover and cook over low heat for one hour, stirring occasionally.

Salt to taste
3 or 4 drops olive oil
Boiling water
½ box of lasagne, 6 oz.
1 recipe meat sauce (given above)
2 packs Mozzarella cheese, grated big (use solid hunk packs)
1 carton Ricotta cheese, cut in small cubes
Italian cheese, grated (enough to cover top of baking dish)
(Romano cheese)

PROCEDURE:

To rapidly boiling water, add salt and olive oil; gradually add lasagne so that water continues to boil. When tender, drain in colander. Use an oblong pyrex or corning ware baking dish 12 x 7½ x 2 inches. Divide grated Mozzarella cheese into three parts, but make the last part to be used for top **much more** than other two parts. **Wait** to put the third top layer on because it browns too fast and will get hard if overcooked. Make three layers in this order with: meat sauce, ⅓ of lasagne, and Mozzarella cheese and ⅓ of Ricotta cheese. After three layers are made, finish using the remaining meat sauce over last layer and sprinkle Italian cheese (Romano) over top. Bake in a moderately preheated oven at 350 degrees for 20 to 25 minutes. Remove from oven and put the third top layer of Mozzarella cheese (biggest part). Cover the entire top with cheese, and bake an additional 15 minutes or until slightly golden brown.

Anna Whittle

BAKED LASAGNE

INGREDIENTS:

¼ **cup olive oil**
½ **cup butter**
½ **cup chopped onions**
4 **toes chopped garlic**
½ **cup finely chopped celery**
.3 **tablespoons cut parsley**
½ **pound ground meat**
½ **teaspoon sugar**

1 **small can tomato paste**
1 **small can tomato sauce**
2 **tablespoons dinner wine**
½ **teaspoon salt**
½ **teaspoon pepper**
1 **pound Mozzarella cheese**
1 - 6 **ounce package grated Parmesan and Romano cheese**
1 **package lasagne**

PROCEDURE:

In wide skillet, to which the butter and olive oil have been placed, (reserve 1 tablespoon of olive oil) add the onions, garlic, and meat. Saute' for 10 minutes. Add tomato contents and celery; sprinkle on the sugar and parsley, cook additional 10 minutes. Add wine, salt, pepper. Cover and continue cooking over low heat for 35 to 40 minutes. Stir occasionally. Set aside. To 3 quarts boiling salted water (2 tablespoons salt) add remaining olive oil. Lower lasagne pieces into water, one by one, cook until pliable. Drain. Cover bottom of rectangular baking dish with ⅓ of the sauce; place lasagne pieces on sauce, then cover with strips of Mozzarella cheese. Continue layer process to completion. Top with generous sprinkling of Parmesan - Romano cheese. Bake for 30 minutes at 375 degrees. Divide into square serving sections. Serves 8.

Deborah Falgoust

LASAGNE

INGREDIENTS:

¼ pound American cheese
¼ pound Swiss cheese
¼ pound ham, cut small
¼ pound cooked Salami, cut small
1 large box of lasagne
1 pound Ricotta cheese
2 pounds ground meat
1 teaspoon oregano
1 package Mozzarella cheese

1 can Italian cheese
1½ gallons water
1 pound Italian sausage
2 cans tomato paste
2 cans puree
4 onions, chopped fine
1 bunch green onions, chopped fine
½ bunch parsley, chopped fine

PROCEDURE:

SAUCE: Fry onions until brown. Add green onions and parsley. Add tomato paste. Cook for ½ hour. Add puree. Cook for ½ hour. Add water, oregano, salt and pepper to taste. Place ground meat in bowl, take skin off of Italian sausage and mix with ground meat. Break up mixture when placing in sauce.

MACARONI: Cook macaroni for 15 minutes in boiling salted water. Take off fire and place in sink, run cold water into pot. Then take macaroni and place in pan in strips. On bottom place a little gravy, then add macaroni in strips till covered ... then gravy. Add American cheese and Swiss cheese to cover layer. Sprinkle Italian cheese. Add another layer macaroni and sauce ... then add a layer of ham and salami. Sprinkle Italian cheese. Next add another layer of macaroni and gravy. Make a layer of Ricotta cheese. Sprinkle Italian cheese. Add another layer of macaroni and gravy. Place Mozzarella cheese and sprinkle Italian cheese on top. Bake in oven at 350 degrees for 2 hours. Serves 6 - 8.

Carol Lirette

LASAGNE

PASTA

2 eggs
1 pound flour
1 tablespoon olive oil

½ teaspoon salt
½ to 1 cup water

PROCEDURE:

Make a well with the flour and add eggs, salt and oil. Start mixing. Add the water a little at a time while continuing to mix dough. After dough is roughly thrown together, either knead dough by hand or by machine. If machine is used to knead dough, begin by setting the roller opening to the maximum setting. Pass the dough through twice. Continue passing the dough through progressively lowering settings. Make sure dough is well floured at all times. Before passing the dough through the machine, divide it into workable quantities.

SAUCE:

1 pound of ground meat (more or less if desired)
1½ to 2 onions (chopped fine or grated)
2 to 3 cloves garlic
1 to 1½ teaspoons of basil
1 bay leaf
½ teaspoon oregano
salt and pepper to taste
3 1 pound cans Progresso peeled tomatoes
sugar

PROCEDURE:

Saute' onions and garlic until brown. Add ground meat. Continue cooking until meat is well browned. Remove pan from heat and set aside. Drain all excess grease from pan. Puree tomatoes in blender. Add tomatoes to meat mixture. Add remaining ingredients and cook sauce over medium flame. Cook for 1 hour. Taste. Add enough sugar (1 teaspoon at a time) to remove "acidy" taste. Allow the sauce to cook for a few minutes before adding additional sugar -- taste again. (additional of the above spices may be used if necessary).

FILLING:

3 pounds of whole Ricotta   **1 egg**
2 or 3 boxes, chopped frozen spinach   **Grated cheese (Italian)**

Parboil the spinach. Drain spinach, making sure to remove all excess water. Mix spinach and Ricotta together in a large bowl. Add the egg. Add Italian cheese. Mix well.

PROCEDURE:

In a large pot add 4 or more quarts of water. Add salt, bring water to boil. Add 1 tablespoon of cooking oil. Add the pasta. When pasta rises to the surface of the water, it should be cooked. Remove pasta from water and drain.

Use a large baking pan for assembling lasagne. First add enough sauce to the bottom of pan to lightly cover it. Next add a row of pasta. Now add sufficient filling to cover pasta, next add more sauce, sprinkle grated cheese over sauce. Add another row of pasta and continue alternating layers. The last layer on top should be pasta, sauce and cheese. Cover pan with aluminum foil. Bake for 45 minutes at

350 degrees. Remove pan from oven. Additional sauce may be added to top of lasagne before serving.

Maria De Francesch
Eliana De Francesch

SAUSAGE LASAGNE

INGREDIENTS:

1 pound hot Italian sausage
1 pound mild Italian sausage
¾ cup chopped onion
2 cloves garlic, minced
1 tablespoon olive oil or
   vegetable oil
1 can (28 oz.) whole tomatoes
1 can (8 oz.) tomato sauce
1 can (6 oz.) tomato paste
2 tablespoons snipped parsley
1 tablespoon salt
1 teaspoon sugar
1 tablespoon dried basil leaves

¼ teaspoon pepper
8 ounces lasagna noodles
1 tablespoon olive oil or vegetable oil
2 teaspoons salt
4 quarts boiling water
1 pound Ricotta cheese
2 egg yolks
2 tablespoons snipped parsley
1 teaspoon salt
¼ teaspoon pepper
¾ pound Mozzarella cheese, sliced
½ cup grated Romano cheese

PROCEDURE:

1. Remove casing from Italian sausage. Cook and stir sausage in skillet over medium heat until brown. Drain.

2. Cook and stir onion and garlic in 1 tablespoon oil in dutch oven, high heat until hot, about 3 minutes. Stir in sausage, tomatoes, tomato sauce, tomato paste, 2 tablespoons parsley, the basil, 1 teaspoon salt, the sugar and ¼ teaspoon pepper. Heat to boiling; reduce heat. Simmer uncovered until mixture is consistency of spaghetti sauce, about 1 hour.

3. Add lasagne noodles to 1 tablespoon oil and 2 teaspoon salt to the boiling water. Boil gently until noodles are tender, 10 to 12 minutes. Drain; rinse with cold water.

4. Mix Ricotta cheese, egg yolks, 2 tablespoons parsley, 1 teaspoon salt and ¼ teaspoon pepper.

5. Heat oven to 350 degrees. Pour one third of the meat sauce into greased baking dish, 13½ x 8¾ x 1¼ inches. Layer half each of the noodles, the remaining meat sauce, the Ricotta cheese mixture and the Mozzarella cheese on top. Repeat layering. Sprinkle with Romano cheese, bake uncovered 45 minutes. Let stand 15 minutes before cutting. Makes 10 to 12 servings.

Mrs. Josie McGinnis

STUFFED JUMBO SHELLS

INGREDIENTS:

1 box frozen chopped spinach
½ pound Ricotta cheese
1-3 ounce package Philadelphia cream cheese
1 pack Ronzoni jumbo shells (12 ounce)
Parmesan cheese
Dash cayenne pepper
Spaghetti sauce (about 2 cups)

PROCEDURE:

Cook spinach as directed on package. Drain. Mix Ricotta cheese, Philadelphia cream cheese, seasoning and spinach.

Boil shells as directed on box. Fill cooked shells with filling.

Cover bottom of baking dish with spaghetti sauce. Arrange filled shells in single layer in dish. Ladle sauce over shells, sprinkle with Parmesan cheese and bake in oven at 350 degrees for about 30 minutes.

Dolores Zaccaria

INSIDE-OUT RAVIOLI

INGREDIENTS:

1 pound ground beef
½ cup chopped onions
1 clove garlic (minced)
1 - 10 ounce package frozen spinach
1 - 1 pound can spaghetti with mushrooms
1 - 7 ounce package (2 cups) shell or elbow
   macaroni (cooked and drained)
1 cup shredded sharp process American cheese

1 8-ounce tomato sauce
1 6-ounce tomato paste
½ teaspoon salt
Dash pepper
½ cup soft bread crumbs
2 well-beaten eggs
¼ cup salad oil

PROCEDURE:

Brown the beef, onions, and garlic in large skillet. Cook spinach using package directions. Drain, reserving liquid. Add enough water to liquid to make one cup. Add spinach liquid and the spaghetti with mushrooms, tomato sauce, tomato paste, salt and pepper, to meat mixture. Simmer ten minutes. Combine spinach with macaroni and remaining ingredients. Spread in 13 x 9 x 2 inch baking dish. Top with meat sauce, bake at 350 degrees for 30 minutes. Let it stand 10 minutes before serving. This serves 8 to 10 persons.

Josie Rhodes

RAVIOLI

INGREDIENTS:
Step 1 - Tomato Gravy

1 - 6 ounce can tomato paste
1 small can tomato sauce
1 tablespoon sugar
3 or 4 cans water
1 small onion (fresh or dehydrated)

3 pieces garlic or garlic powder
1 tablespoon parsley
1 teaspoon bell pepper
small amount of sweet basil

Make gravy the same way as spaghetti sauce recipe. Hold aside.

Step 2 - Meat stuffing mixture

1 pound ground meat
1 or 2 tablespoons onion, chopped
1 clove or piece garlic or garlic powder

1 tablespoon parsley
salt and pepper to taste

Fry ground meat loose; drain off excess grease, then add all seasoning, salt and pepper. Hold aside.

Step 3 - Parboil big macaroni (Tufoli or Manicotti) in water and **little** olive oil to keep from sticking while boiling for about 8 to 10 minutes, drain well. Hold aside.

Step 4 - Big macaroni
Meat stuffing mixture
Italian cheese, grated

Mozzarella cheese, grated
Ricotta cheese, small pieces

Stuff big macaroni with meat stuffing mixture, put gravy and sprinkle above ingredients, except Mozzarella cheese alternately in an oblong pyrex or corning ware baking pan. Bake at 350 degrees for 35 minutes and 5 minutes before done, sprinkle grated Mozzarella cheese over top. If it looks like it's getting dry while baking, put a cover over it (aluminum foil if pan has no cover) for about 15 minutes of baking time.

Anna Whittle

DRUNKMAN'S BREAKFAST

INGREDIENTS:

6 eggs or amount needed
1 large onion, chopped
1 large can crushed tomatoes
¼ cup olive oil

1 tablespoon sugar
1 tablespoon salt
½ teaspoon black pepper
1 cup water

PROCEDURE:

Saute' onions in olive oil, do not brown. Add tomatoes, sugar and water. Season to taste. Simmer 10 minutes. Make a well in sauce for each egg and drop into mixture. Sprinkle eggs with salt and pepper. Cover and let simmer for 5 minutes or until eggs are poached.

Katie Ceravolo

SPAGHETTI SAUCE WITH
MEATBALLS AND EGGPLANT

INGREDIENTS:

2 cans tomato paste
3 cans tomato sauce
3 toes garlic
2 medium onions
1 small green pepper
1 large eggplant
2 pounds spaghetti

2 pounds ground meat
1 cup bread crumbs
3 eggs
¼ cup grated Parmesan cheese
1 tablespoon parsley
½ cup milk
Salt and pepper to taste

PROCEDURE:

SAUCE: Saute' onions, pepper, and garlic in olive oil. Add tomato paste and sauce -- fry for a few minutes. Add about 1 quart of water. Season to taste. Simmer 2 hours. Add 1 teaspoon sugar or a pinch of baking soda to gravy. Combine ground meat, bread crumbs, eggs, cheese, parsley, milk and seasoning. Mix well. Shape into meatballs and fry until brown on both sides. Add to gravy and simmer another hour. Slice or cube eggplant. Sprinkle with salt and let stand ½ hour. Rinse in water and drop into sauce with meatballs. Serve over cooked spaghetti.

Theresa Frickey

TAGLIARINI

INGREDIENTS:

4 cups flour
4 eggs
2 tablespoons olive oil

PROCEDURE:

Make a well in flour. Add eggs and oil and mix well. Work dough with the heel of the hand until stiff and elastic, adding more flour if needed. Cut dough in four parts and roll out each part on floured board as thin as possible. Set aside and let dry. Fold each sheet like a jelly roll and cut into strips ¼ to ½ inch wide. Pick up strips and shake loose. Cook about five minutes in 4 quarts salted boiling water. Drain well and serve with tomato sauce and grated Romano cheese.

Grace Panepinto

CLAMS LINGUINE

INGREDIENTS:

3 tablespoons olive oil
2 tablespoons butter
2 cloves garlic, cut in halves
½ cup finely minced onions
1 large can Italian tomatoes
1 bag linguine
1 teaspoon oregano

1 teaspoon salt
½ teaspoon pepper
¼ teaspoon sugar
1 bay leaf
1 cup finely cut parsley
2 dozen clams, free of all shells
1 cup strained clam water

PROCEDURE:

Place garlic pieces in heated olive oil. Cook over medium heat in wide, heavy skillet for 5 to 10 minutes. Remove from heat and discard garlic. Place onions, tomatoes, salt, pepper, sugar, bay leaf and oregano in original olive oil. Mix well, cover and cook on medium heat for 25 to 30 minutes. Stir often to completely blend flavor. Remove bay leaf and discard. Add parsley, butter, clams and clam water. Stir well, recover and bring to simmering stage. Cook for 10 minutes longer. Serve over 1 pound of hot linguine or noodles. Serves 6 (may be sprinkled with grated Parmesan or Romano cheese).

Deborah Falgoust

ARTICHOKE LINGUINE

INGREDIENTS:

¼ cup olive oil
½ stick butter
1 tablespoon flour
1¼ cup chicken stock
1 garlic clove, crushed
2 teaspoons lemon juice

1 tablespoon minced parsley
salt and pepper to taste
1 can artichokes - drained
　(cut each artichoke in 4 pieces)
1 tablespoon drained capers
2 tablespoons Italian cheese

PROCEDURE:

Heat oil and butter - add flour - cook for 3 minutes. Stir in chicken stock - cook 1 minute more. Add garlic, lemon juice, parsley, salt and pepper -- cook 5 minutes on low heat while stirring occasionally. Add artichoke and Italian cheese, stir -- add capers, cook for another 5 to 8 minutes. Set aside, covered.

Cook 1 pound linguine -- drain - return cooked linguine to bowl and add 2 tablespoons olive oil, ¼ cup Italian cheese and ½ stick melted butter -- mix well. Serve lingiune topped with the artichoke sauce. Serves 4 to 5.

Josie Belletto

BECHAMEL SAUCE

INGREDIENTS:

4 tablespoons butter
¼ cup flour
2½ cups milk (boiling hot)
salt and pepper to taste
Variation: Add 1 or 2 cups of lump crabmeat (fresh)
Grated Parmesan or Romano cheese

PROCEDURE:

In a small saucepan, melt butter over gentle heat. Add flour, and using a wooden spoon, stir and cook without browning for several minutes. Remove from heat, and stir in milk little by little, mixing to a smooth sauce. Stir until boiling then simmer for 10 minutes. Season to taste with salt and pepper. (a little nutmeg won't hurt) omit nutmeg if using crab meat. Don't forget to top pasta and sauce with cheese.

Antoinette Maselli

POLENTA WITH MUSHROOM SAUCE

INGREDIENTS:

(see below)
PROCEDURE: **For the sauce:**

Put in a casserole ½ cup butter and 4 tablespoons of olive oil at low flame; when it is hot add 1 chopped onion, 2 chopped carrots, 1 chopped stalk of celery and 5 ounces chopped mushrooms (dried). Cook 5 minutes or until onion is melted. Add 1 cup canned Italian plum tomatoes and ½ cup dry white wine. Bring to a boil. Cover and cook over low heat, stirring occasionally. When ready, top with sauteed, sliced fresh mushrooms and sprinkle with chopped parsley. Serve with Polenta.

For the Polenta:

In top of double boiler, bring 1 quart of water to a boil over direct heat. Add 1¼ teaspoon salt and gradually stir in 1 cup of yellow corn -meal. Place over hot water and cook for half hour, stirring constantiy. Serve with the above mentioned sauce. (To save time, Instant Polenta may be used as directed). Serves 4.

Colette Bosco

Cheeses

GRATING CHEESES

PARMIGIANO REGGIANO, the original Italian Parmesan, is a salty and sharp cheese.

PECORINO ROMANO is a sharp cheese made of fresh sheep's milk curdled with lamb's rennet.

TABLE CHEESES

TALEGGIO, has a slightly aromatic flavor.

FONTINA is a sweet and delicate cheese.

PROVOLONE is a delicate and creamy cheese.

ASIAGO, sharp but palatable, is hard and granular and is made from two cow milkings.

GORGONZOLA is a lightly spiced and sharp cheese.

BEL PAESE is a smooth and daintily flavored cheese.

COOKING CHEESES

RICOTTA is a fresh, moist, unsalted variety of cottage cheese.

MOZZARELLA is a pleasant, slightly sour cheese.

Vegetables & Casseroles

CARCIOFI ALLA ROMANA
(Artichokes Roman Style)

INGREDIENTS:

8 medium artichokes
Juice of large lemon
⅓ cup bread crumbs
8 anchovy fillets, chopped
5 leaves minced mint

1 teaspoon salt
2 cups water
½ cup olive oil
4 tablespoons parsley
½ teaspoon dried mint

PROCEDURE:

Cut off stalks and tips of artichokes and remove tougher outer leaves. Press artichokes down, holding them by the stems to spread leaves. With small sharp knife remove spiny chokes, if necessary. Place the artichokes in bowl of water to which lemon juice has been added. Mix together bread crumbs, anchovies, parsley, mint and pepper. Moisten with enough water or oil to make a paste. Drain artichokes and fill the centers with the mixture. Place in saucepan, add water, salt and oil, cover tightly and cook slowly for 30 to 45 minutes, depending on tenderness of artichokes. May be eaten hot or cold. Serves 4.

Colette Bosco

STUFFED ARTICHOKES

INGREDIENTS:

1 large can redi-mix crumbs
1½ cups grated Italian cheese
1 medium onion chopped fine
5 toes garlic chopped fine
2 ribs celery chopped fine

1 teaspoon salt
1½ teaspoons oregano
1½ teaspoons poultry seasoning
1½ teaspoons thyme
½ cup finely chopped parsley

29

PROCEDURE:

Fill large pot ¾ full with water. Add 3 ribs of celery, 1 onion, 4 toes garlic, 1 lemon cut in half, 1 hot pepper, 2 teaspoons thyme, oregano, poultry seasoning and 2 tablespoons salt. Place artichokes (tops cut off and stems and leaves trimmed) in water and boil for about 20 minutes. Drain and fill with stuffing.

STUFFING FOR 6 ARTICHOKES:

Mix all ingredients together well. Add ¾ cup olive oil and mix thoroughly. Fill artichokes with mixture. Add slice of lemon to top of each and wrap tightly in aluminum foil. Steam in 2'' water for 2 hours, covered well.

Mercedes Romano

STUFFED ARTICHOKES

INGREDIENTS:

6 artichokes	3 strands parsley
1 large onion	1 cup grated Italian cheese
6 toes garlic	1 large can Italian bread crumbs
3 strips shallots	olive oil

PROCEDURE:

Cut the tops off of artichokes about 1½ inches from top, then cut the bottom stem. Wash artichokes and drain. Chop all of the seasoning. Put in a large bowl, and mix all the ingredients except the olive oil. Then put an artichoke in the middle of your pan and stuff each leaf, if you can. After you have stuffed all of the artichokes, put about 1 inch of slightly salted water in a large pot or pan with a lid and place the artichokes in it. Pour about 2 tablespoons of olive oil over each one. Now place on medium fire and cook for 1½ to 2 hours or until a leaf can be pulled out easily. Never let the water cook off the artichokes. Add more water in the pot as it boils down. The slightly salted water salts the hearts.

Lorraine Taravella

STUFFED ARTICHOKES IN ITALIAN GRAVY

INGREDIENTS:

Basic Italian tomato gravy	Pot large enough to hold 6 artichokes
6 artichokes	3 pounds ground meat
3 eggs	salt and pepper to taste
1 onion, finely chopped	1 cup each of grated cheese and progresso bread crumbs

Clean artichokes, cut off stem and at least ¼ inch off of top, trim each leaf. Mix ground meat and other ingredients well. Stuff between leaves of artichokes with prepared ground meat. After each artichoke is stuffed, place in Italian gravy, stem up. Let cook 3½ to 4 hours on low fire. Serve with spaghetti. Serves 6.

Ruby Armbruster

ARTICHOKES STUFFED WITH FAVA BEANS AND BACON

INGREDIENTS:

4 artichokes
4 lemon slices and 2 teaspoons lemon juice
1 teaspoon garlic salt or 2 cloves garlic
1 teaspoon olive oil
1 teaspoon salt
¼ teaspoon pepper
½ cup grated Italian cheese
½ pound bacon
½ pound fava beans or 1 can fava beans
7-ounces Italian bread crumbs

PROCEDURE:

Wash artichokes, trim stem ends, pull off tough outer leaves and snip off tips of remaining leaves. Place artichokes upside down, press down firmly. Remove center leaves and choke. Place artichokes in salt water and wash;

Fry Bacon and crumble into bacon bits;

Mix together - bread crumbs, garlic, olive oil, salt, pepper, Italian cheese, bacon, fava beans;

Fill artichokes with this mixture;

Top with lemon slice. Place in 1 inch boiling water, add lemon juice, salt, pepper to water, cover. Cook 35 to 45 minutes (depending upon size) or until a leaf pulls away easily from base. Pour olive oil over each artichoke. Serves 4.

Dolores Zaccaria

ARTICHOKE HEARTS WITH GROUND MEAT

INGREDIENTS:

2 cans artichoke hearts
2 pounds ground meat
1½ cups Italian bread crumbs
½ cup olive oil

½ cup grated Romano cheese
¼ each teaspoon garlic powder
salt and pepper

PROCEDURE:

Fry ground meat well, drain off excess fat, cut artichoke hearts in four, save liquid. Mix remaining ingredients well, add artichoke hearts and liquid, olive oil last, mix well. Bake at 350 degrees for 30 to 40 minutes. Serves 6 - 8.

Frances Falcone East

ARTICHOKE and MACARONI CASSEROLE

INGREDIENTS:

1 box (8 ounce) elbow macaroni
1 cup green onion, chopped
1 large onion, chopped
½ cup parsley
1 teaspoon oregano
8 ounces olive oil

1 cup milk
1 can artichoke hearts
1 cup Italian bread crumbs
1 cup plain bread crumbs
1 box Ricotta cheese
1 pound Parmesan cheese

PROCEDURE:

Boil macaroni, mix all above ingredients together with milk and mashed artichoke hearts. Then mix with macaroni, put in a casserole dish and top with cheese, cover and bake till all the cheese is melted.

Lena Ford

ARTICHOKES AND PEAS

INGREDIENTS:

1 large can 8/10 count artichoke hearts,
  quarter and drain
1 8-ounce can peas, drained
2 to 3 tablespoons olive oil

2 cloves garlic, minced
1 tablespoon parsley, chopped
salt and pepper to taste

PROCEDURE:

Heat olive oil; add garlic. Saute' until golden brown. Add parsley, salt and pepper, and artichoke hearts; saute' for 5 minutes. Add peas and simmer on slow heat for 5 minutes or longer and serve hot. Serves 6 to 8.

Marie Gattuso

ARTICHOKE CASSEROLE

INGREDIENTS:

2 cans artichoke - cut in pieces
1 bag (12 ounce) elbow macaroni
  (boiled)
1 cup Italian bread crumbs
½ cup Italian cheese
8 ounces pure olive oil

Salt, pepper, and oregano to taste
4 toes garlic, chopped
1 egg and 1 cup milk (beaten together)
1 bunch shallots (chopped)
1 onion (chopped)
½ cup parsley (chopped)

PROCEDURE:

Mix and bake in 2 quart casserole dish uncovered for 35 to 45 minutes at 350 degrees. Serves 6.

Carolyn Hornyak

ASPARAGI IN FRITTATA

INGREDIENTS:

½ bunch fresh asparagus
5 eggs
½ pound Ricotta cheese

Salt and pepper
¼ cup olive oil

PROCEDURE:

Cook asparagus in small amount of salted water until done. Drain and set aside. Beat eggs. Add ricotta, salt and pepper and blend well. Cut asparagus in 2 inch pieces and add to mixture. Heat oil over high flame in large oven-proof skillet. Carefully pour egg mixture into pan. Fry over medium heat for about 10 minutes, loosening sides of frittata with spatula. Remove skillet from flame and place under medium broiler for 5 minutes or until golden brown. Remove from broiler, place large platter over skillet and carefully turn over, depositing frittata on plate. Serve hot or cold to 7 or 8 persons.

Grace Panepinto

ITALIAN SAUSAGE and BROCCOLI CASSEROLE

INGREDIENTS:

1 package frozen broccoli (chopped)
2 cups wine (white)
½ cup Italian bread crumbs
12 links Italian sausage

Cheese sauce:
Equal amounts of Italian cheese (8 ounce). American cheese (8 ounce) 1½ cups milk, 1 teaspoon flour, ½ stick butter. Salt and pepper to taste.

PROCEDURE:

Cook sausage in wine until almost done. Add 1 package broccoli. Finish cooking on low heat until broccoli is tender. While this is simmering make cheese sauce:

Melt cheese and butter in saucepan; slowly adding milk with flour, salt and pepper, mixing until flour is dissolved. Arrange drained broccoli and sausage in shallow baking dish in shape of a pinwheel. Pour cheese sauce over top, sprinkle with bread crumbs. Bake until cheese starts to brown. Serve hot with garlic bread. Serves 6.   350 degrees

Helen Cannaliato

BROCCOLI — RICE CASSEROLE

INGREDIENTS:

2 cups cooked rice
3 tablespoons butter
1 box frozen chopped broccoli
1 can cream of chicken soup
1 soup can of milk

1 small jar of cheese whiz
1 cup chopped onions
1 cup chopped celery
salt and pepper

PROCEDURE:

Thaw broccoli in 1 cup of boiling water. Saute' onions and celery in butter. Add soup and soup can of milk to onions and celery. Then add cheese whiz. Simmer for a minute or so, then add thawed broccoli, rice and salt and pepper. Bake 30 to 40 minutes or so in oven about 350 to 375 degrees. This recipe can be made ahead of time.

Rita Phillip

LILLIAN'S STUFFED EGGPLANT

INGREDIENTS:

1 large eggplant
1 egg
1 large onion
Thyme, bay leaf, parsley
1 cup chopped shrimp

1 cup Italian bread crumbs
1 or 2 fresh tomatoes
2 cloves garlic
2 tablespoons olive oil
salt and pepper to taste

PROCEDURE:

Cut eggplant in half and boil until tender. Drain and cool. Scoop out center carefully. Chop eggplant center that has been scooped, fine. Mix in bread crumbs, egg, salt, pepper and shrimp. Chop onion and garlic fine. Brown slightly in olive oil. Add chopped tomatoes and its juice. Cook 5 minutes -- add minced herbs and eggplant mixture. Fill eggplant shells. Sprinkle crumbs and Italian cheese over top. Dot with butter and brown at 350 degrees.

Lillian Ferroni Newton

EGGPLANT PANCAKES

INGREDIENTS:

2 eggplants
1 cup Italian bread crumbs
½ cup grated Italian cheese
1 toe garlic (slivered)

1 small onion (chopped fine)
1 large egg
salt and pepper to taste
flour

PROCEDURE:

Peel, cube and boil eggplant until tender. Drain and mash. Mix eggplant with next 6 ingredients. Roll in flour and shape into pancakes. Heat teflon coated griddle, which has been slightly oiled. Cook about 5 minutes on each side or until done.

Dolores Zaccaria

EGG PLANT PARMIGIANO

INGREDIENTS:

3 small to medium eggplants
2½ cups seasoned Italian bread crumbs
(add: sweet basil, salt, pepper, salted Italian cheese to taste)
4 whole eggs, 1 ounce milk beaten together
1 package sliced Mozzarella cheese (6 or 8 ounces)

PROCEDURE:

Peel and slice egg plants into medium slices. Set aside to drain. Dip each slice of eggplant into egg mixture, then into bread crumbs. Bread both sides. Re-dip into eggs and bread crumb mixture. Fry each slice in hot cooking oil. Lightly brown both sides. Place layer of cooked eggplant into deep baking dish, cover with layer of Mozzarella cheese. Continue with layer of each and top with the cheese. Pour approximately 2 cups of Italian sauce over entire dish. Place cover and cook in preheated oven at 350 degrees for about ½ hour or about 45 minutes if eggplants have been prepared and cooked ahead of time. Serves approximately 5 people very generously.

Lena R. Ales

EGGPLANT PARMESAN

INGREDIENTS FOR GRAVY:

3 cans paste (small)

6 cans sauce (small)

6 cloves of garlic

1 tablespoon oregano

1 tablespoon thyme

2 tablespoons sugar

1 tablespoon sweet basil or if available

   fresh sweet basil leaves

   (usually about 6 leaves)

salt and pepper to taste

(Remember half will be used over your spaghetti and the other half will be used in casserole)

INGREDIENTS FOR EGGPLANT:

1 large or 2 small eggplants

salt and pepper

sugar

cooking oil

sweet basil

PROCEDURE:

First prepare Italian gravy. Use two (2) cans of sauce to one (1) can of paste. Chop onions very fine and saute' same in a small amount of cooking oil until limp but not brown. To this add paste and stir constantly over low heat until paste starts to hold together and turns dark red or brownish red. To this add garlic cloves (whole), sweet basil, thyme, oregano and sugar. Continue to stir and saute mixture for about fifteen minutes. At this time add sauce to mixture and stir and saute until you can see mixture has blended and is rather thick. At this time you may add your water for the consistency you desire. (Usually two (2) cans of water for every can of paste and can of sauce used.) Add salt and pepper to taste.

(OPTIONAL) At this point you may add pork, beef meatballs or sausage, if you so desire.

This should be allowed to cook at least three hours over medium heat. Be careful to check pot to see if additional water may be needed. If so, add to mixture and continue to cook for required time.

While gravy is cooking, peel one (1) to two (2) eggplants depending on the size of same. Either 1 large or 2 small. Slice same lengthwise and rather thin, salt heavily and stack in plate. They will then produce a water syrup. Allow them to stand for at least one half hour. Rinse thoroughly and pat dry on paper towels. Then fry lightly on both sides in small amount of cooking oil. Be sure to let fried eggplant drain once more on paper towels. Next, layer bottom of lightly buttered casserole dish with gravy, then eggplant, then Italian cheese. Keep on layering until you reach inch from top of casserole dish, being sure that last layer is cheese. (BEFORE YOU START YOUR LAYER PROCESS BE SURE THAT YOU LIGHTLY SALT AND PEPPER AND SPRINKLE BOTH SIDES OF EACH PIECE OF EGGPLANT

WITH SUGAR. (THIS IS A VERY IMPORTANT FLAVOR SECRET). ALSO IF AVAILABLE, ADD FRESH SWEET BASIL BETWEEN LAYERS AFTER EACH EGGPLANT LAYER. IF THIS IS NOT AVAILABLE SPRINKLE DRIED PREPARED SWEET BASIL BETWEEN LAYERS)

Cover and cook eggplant casserole in oven at 350 degrees for approximately one and one-half (1½) hours. Serve over spaghetti. Serves 4 to 6 people.

Vivian C. Mendoza

EGGPLANT AND SHRIMP

INGREDIENTS:

5 small eggplants
2 pounds cleaned small shrimp
1 medium onion, chopped fine
½ medium bell pepper, chopped fine
½ teaspoon salt

½ cup bread crumbs
2 tablespoons Italian cheese
 (Romano)
2 tablespoons chopped parsley
dash black pepper
dash oregano

PROCEDURE:

Simmer eggplant halves in salted water (boiling) until tender, about 15 minutes. Drain and scoop out pulp -- save outer skin. Set aside. Mix cheese and bread crumbs together. Set aside.

Saute' onions and bell pepper in oil or butter until golden brown, add shrimp and cook until tender, then add eggplant pulp, stirring over medium heat until well mixed. Season with salt, black pepper, parsley and oregano and half of bread crumb mixture. Fill eggplant shells with the above dressing and sprinkle each half with remaining bread crumb mixture. Bake in butter greased pan for 20 minutes. Serve warm. Serves 5.

Alice Randazzo

EGGPLANT SANDWICHES

3 medium eggplants

Peel and slice lengthwise ½ inch thick. Soak in heavily salted water for ½ hour; squeeze water out of slices being careful not to break them.

Filling:

1 pound lean ground meat and
¼ pound chopped ham
1 tablespoon Italian cheese (grated)
3 heaping tablespoons bread crumbs

1 tablespoon parsley, minced
1 or 2 tablespoons onion, minced
1 teaspoon garlic, minced
2 raw eggs
salt and pepper to taste

37

PROCEDURE:

Mix filling together. Put raw filling between two slices of raw eggplant. Dip in beaten eggs and then roll in mixture of bread crumbs (½ Italian and ½ plain) and one teaspoon Italian cheese. Fry in a generous amount of hot cooking oil with cover on a medium fire. Fry until real brown. Drain on paper towels.

Gravy

2 cans tomato sauce
2 cans water
very little sweet basil (about ¼ teaspoon)
1 tablespoon chopped onions

Mix all together and cook on medium heat for about ½ hour. The cooked eggplant sandwiches should be placed in a pot and cooked in the gravy for about another 20 minutes.

Variation:

1 pound of peeled shrimp may be used in place of ground meat and ham in this recipe.

Anna Whittle

ITALIAN CAULIFLOWER

INGREDIENTS:

1 medium cauliflower
2 eggs well beaten
½ cup cream
½ cup sifted all purpose flour

salt and pepper to taste
olive oil for frying
grated parmesan cheese

PROCEDURE:

Wash and trim cauliflower, break into flowerets, mix egg, cream and salt and pepper to taste. Dip cauliflower into liquid mixture then into flour. (Fry in hot olive oil, serve hot with grated Parmesan cheese on top.)

Betty Monfra

FRIED STRING BEANS

INGREDIENTS:

2 cans string beans
seasoned bread crumbs
garlic powder
2 eggs
2 onions, chopped

olive oil
½ cup Italian cheese
salt
pepper

PROCEDURE:

Place beans in boiling water. Drain in collander. Mix in bowl - bread crumbs, garlic powder, salt and pepper. Place in frying pan with olive oil. (add sauted onions if desired) Beat eggs and pour over beans. Mix in Italian cheese. Cook slowly on top of stove, turning as necessary.

Rose Mary Lockhart

KATHY'S GREENBEAN CASSEROLE

INGREDIENTS:

2 large cans french cut string beans (drained)
   (reserve ¼ cup juice)
1 cup Italian bread crumbs   ¼ cup olive oil
1 cup Romano cheese   ¼ cup juice from beans
6 cloves garlic, finely chopped   ¼ cup lemon juice

PROCEDURE:

Mix wet ingredients, mix dry ingredients. Drain beans, reserving ¼ cup liquid. Place 1 layer green beans in casserole dish, sprinkle ⅓ dry mixture over beans, then ⅓ wet mixture. Make 2 more layers of same. Sprinkle a little more cheese over top and bake 25 to 30 minutes at 325 degrees. Serves 8.

Mrs. Patricia De Martini, Sr.

STUFFED MIRLITONS

INGREDIENTS:

3 mirlitons   ½ teaspoon thyme, minced
1 onion, chopped   1 bay leaf
1 clove garlic, chopped   1½ dozen shrimp, cut in two
1 tablespoon butter or margarine   ¾ cup Italian bread crumbs
1 tomato, chopped   salt and pepper to taste
1 sprig parsley, chopped

PROCEDURE:

Cut mirlitons in half and put into salted boiling water. Boil until tender. Remove and cool. Scoop out the tender pulp, remove seeds and mash. Reserve mirliton shells. Brown onion, and garlic in butter or margarine, add tomato, parsley, thyme and bay leaf. Salt and pepper to taste. Fry for 5 minutes, the pulp of the mirliton, (which have been cooked in water and mashed) bread crumbs, and shrimp. Mix well and fill shells with the stuffing. Top with bread crumbs and dot each shell with butter. Place in 350 degree oven and bake for about 15 minutes or until golden brown. Serves 6.

Faith Peperone

FRIED OKRA WITH EGGS

INGREDIENTS:

2 pounds fresh okra
1 small onion, sliced
salt and pepper

cooking oil, small amount
4 eggs, beaten slightly

PROCEDURE:

Wash okra when whole and dry off good with paper towels. Cut ends off, then cut in slices. Fry in oil with onions. Cover while frying and cook until tender and a little brown, add beaten eggs and fry until done. Serves 4.

Anna Whittle

SPINACH A LA FERRONI

INGREDIENTS:

6 slices bacon
1 medium onion
2 packages frozen, chopped spinach
1 cup Italian bread crumbs
2 eggs (beaten)

1 slice ham, chopped
4 toes garlic, chopped fine
1 cup grated Parmesan cheese
  (or Romano)
salt and pepper to taste

PROCEDURE:

Fry bacon in large frying pan until crisp - drain on paper towel, break into medium bits, remove excess grease from pan. Fry onions until lightly done. Add chopped ham just before onions are done. Add spinach and chopped garlic. Cook spinach only until it is defrosted and hot. Mix well. Add bread crumbs, bacon, ham, cheese, eggs, salt and pepper. Cover after mixing - this can be served juicy or can be cooked until set. Takes about 5 minutes to set. Don't over cook. Serves 6.

Lillian Ferroni Newton

ITALIAN SQUASH

INGREDIENTS:

4 fresh tomatoes or 1 can crushed tomatoes
2 toes garlic
3 basil leaves
¼ teaspoon oregano
¼ cup olive oil

salt and pepper to taste
1 large chopped onion
2 cups water
5 pounds squash

PROCEDURE:

Clean squash skin with potato skinner. Dice squash. In large pot, add squash and all of the above ingredients. Cook about 1 hour or until squash is done. Variation: Drop raw eggs in holes made in sauce, cover and cook until eggs are poached. Serves 8.

Katie Ceravolo

HOT SQUASH CASSEROLE

INGREDIENTS:

2 pounds yellow squash
4 ounces green chili peppers
1 medium onion (chopped)
2 whole eggs, beaten well

Italian bread crumbs
1 8-ounce jar cheez whiz
1 can cream of chicken soup
1 teaspoon sugar

(From green pepper, remove seeds and chop fine)

PROCEDURE:

Cut and cube squash. Cook in boiling water until tender and drain well. Spread cheese on bottom of casserole (it rises to top) and mix squash, soup, peppers, onions and eggs. Add salt, pepper and sugar to taste. Top with Italian bread crumbs and bake at 350 degrees for 30 to 40 minutes. Serves 7 to 8.

Esther Stringer

TOMATO AND SQUASH CASSEROLE

INGREDIENTS:

4 summer squash
3 fresh tomatoes
2 medium onions

1 teaspoon salt
½ teaspoon pepper
2 tablespoons butter

PROCEDURE:

Wash and drain squash. Cut into halves, remove seeds. Slice into greased casserole dish, arrange evenly. Slice washed tomatoes to cover squash. Slice onions to cover tomatoes. Sprinkle with salt and pepper. Dot with butter and cover. Bake at 350 degrees for 45 minutes. Serves 6.

Deborah Falgoust

AUNT JENNIE'S ITALIAN SQUASH

INGREDIENTS:

2 dozen small or 1½ dozen large zucchini squash
1 large onion
1 No. 303 can tomatoes
1-6 ounce can tomato paste

2 tablespoons sugar (or to taste)
salt and pepper to taste

PROCEDURE:

Scrape squash and quarter. Dice onion and fry to light brown. Add squash and cook for 5 minutes, turning often. Add remaining ingredients; cook on fast heat until squash are tender. Serves 6.

Rita G. Phillip

VEGETALIAL FORNO
(Baked Vegetables)

INGREDIENTS:

1 eggplant

2 large onions (sliced)

1 zucchini

4 fresh tomatoes

¼ cup olive oil

salt and pepper

¾ pound Mozzarella cheese (sliced)

3 tablelspoons chopped fresh basil

PROCEDURE:

Pare eggplant in-half inch slices. Cut zucchini into quarters in crosswise slices. Do not pare. Grease the bottom of a baking dish with olive oil. Put in a layer of eggplant, a layer of onions, a layer of zucchini, a layer of tomatoes, and layer of cheese. Repeat until all ingredients are used. Pour olive oil over all. Sprinkle with salt and pepper. Bake in moderate 350 degree oven until vegetables are tender and cheese melted. Serves 4.

Grace Panepinto

ITALIAN BAKED POTATOES

INGREDIENTS:

1 medium potato, peeled and diced (per person)

salt and pepper to taste

parsley flakes

Paprika

olive oil

PROCEDURE:

Allow medium potato per person. Place diced potatoes in bowl and add salt, pepper and paprika. Allow approximately 1 tablespoon parsley per 6 potatoes. Toss all together until potatoes are coated. Transfer to a well greased (or pam sprayed) covered casserole dish. Drizzle with oil, about 1 teaspoon per potato. You may use ½ pat of oleo or butter per potato in place of oil. Bake about 1 hour or until potatoes are done and browned a little, 350 to 375 degrees. Can be baked when you bake chicken Parmesan.

Optional: Sprinkle a little garlic powder on potatoes when mixing.

Mae Bingo

ZIP'S FAVE' BEANS

INGREDIENTS:

2 pounds fave' beans
½ cup olive oil
6 pods garlic, chopped fine

2 small onions, chopped fine
8 ounce package vermicelli (spaghetti)
2 quarts water

PROCEDURE:

Saute' onions and garlic in olive oil, add beans and simmer for 10 minutes. Add water and cook for 30 minutes. Separately, cook spaghetti until tender, drain; then add to beans and serve. If desired, sprinkle Italian cheese over beans and spaghetti. Serves 8.

Mrs. Helen Chimento

FAVA BEANS

INGREDIENTS:

1 pound dry fava beans
3 tablespoons olive oil
salt and pepper

PROCEDURE:

Soak beans overnight. Drain and cover with salted water, and cook over low flame until shells are loose -- 2 to 3 hours. Add more water if necessary. Drain. Season with salt and pepper. Add oil and serve hot or cold.

Grace Panepinto

AUNT JENNIE'S ITALIAN RED BEANS

INGREDIENTS:

2 cans (3 pounds, 5 ounce) red kidney beans
2 pounds Italian sausage
1 large onion, finely chopped
4 tablespoons brown sugar (or to taste)
2 cooking spoons of honey
1 No. 303 can tomatoes
1 - 6 ounce can tomato paste
salt and pepper to taste

PROCEDURE:

Cut up and fry sausage. Fry onion to light brown and add sugar, tomatoes, honey, paste and sausage. Cook on fast heat for about 1 hour stirring frequently, until gravy is thick. Add beans and cook for 7 minutes.

Rita G. Phillip

ITALIAN—AMERICAN DIRTY RICE

INGREDIENTS:

No salt
1 can beef bouillon soup   **1 pound Italian or country sausage**
1 can onion soup   **(cut into bite sizes)**
¾ cup water   **1 stick of peperoni, sliced**
1 cup raw rice   **½ block of butter or margarine**
1 - 4½ ounce jar or can sliced mushrooms, drained
               (Remove casing from sausage and peperoni)

PROCEDURE:

After cutting sausage and peperoni up, just mix all ingredients together and bake in a casserole. This is an easy and simple dish to prepare -- and delicious too. Makes 10 generous servings.

Angelina Dugas

Seafood

SHRIMP MOLD

INGREDIENTS:

1½ envelopes unflavored gelatin
1 pound boiled and chopped shrimp
3 small packages cream cheese
1 can tomato soup

1 cup mayonnaise
¾ cup chopped celery
¼ cup onion

PROCEDURE:

Dissolve gelatin in ¼ cup cold water and set aside. Bring soup to boil and dissolve cream cheese. Remove from heat and add the remaining ingredients, then place in mold, and refrigerate.

Mrs. Faith Peperone

MARINATED SHRIMP

INGREDIENTS:

5 pounds shrimp (peeled & deveined)
½ pound butter or margarine
1 cup olive oil
8 ounces chili sauce
3 tablespoons worcestershire sauce
2 lemons (cut and squeezed)
4 cloves garlic

3 tablelspoons lemon juice
1 tablespoon parsley
2 tablespoons paprika
2 tablespoons red pepper
1 tablespoon tabasco
2 dashes liquid smoke
salt and pepper to taste

PROCEDURE:

Mix all ingredients in large pan, add shrimp and marinate overnight. Bake in 300 degree oven for 30 minutes. Serves 6 to 8.

Mrs. Shirley Centanni

SHRIMP MOSCA

INGREDIENTS:

2 pounds headless shrimp in shells
6 buds garlic
2 pieces whole bay leaves
1 teaspoon rosemary
1 teaspoon oregano

1 teaspoon crushed black pepper
1 tablespoon salt
2 ounces olive oil
1 ounce Sauterne wine

PROCEDURE:

Heat oil in large skillet and add all ingredients except wine. Cook for twenty to twenty-five minutes, add wine and saute' an additional ten to fifteen minutes. Serve with lemon wedges and sprigs of parsley for garnish. Serves 4.

Nick Mosca, Chef
Elmwood Plantation

TASTY SHRIMP ITALIAN

INGREDIENTS:

8 pounds raw shrimp, deheaded
1 stick butter
2 big cooking spoons olive oil
1 large onion, chopped
½ small bottle Italian seasoning

salt to taste
crushed red pepper
1 teaspoon minced garlic
1 teaspoon dry parsley
1 tablespoon worcestershire sauce

PROCEDURE:

Soften onion with butter and olive oil. Take off fire, add shrimp and all seasoning; stir, put back on fire. Cover and cook for about 15 or 20 minutes.

Cut recipe in half to make less.

Marie Vicari

CASEY'S SHRIMP

INGREDIENTS:

4 pounds shrimp (remove head and first section of tail)
4 crushed bay leaves
¾ teaspoon oregano
¾ teaspoon rosemary
¾ teaspoon fresh ground pepper
14 whole pepper corns
2½ teaspoons salt

1 teaspoon accent
14 toes garlic (cut into four pieces each)
4 ounces olive oil
3 ounces Sauterne wine
1 stick butter (not margarine)

PROCEDURE:

In large, sealable container combine bay leaves, oregano, rosemary, pepper, pepper corns, salt, accent, garlic and olive oil. Add shrimp, marinate over night. Stir occasionally or turn over so all shrimp marinate equally. Keep in refrigerator. When ready to prepare, melt butter in large skillet, pour shrimp and liquid into butter and saute' for fifteen or twenty minutes until light brown. Add Sauterne and cook ten more minutes, until wine evaporates slightly. Serve with remaining liquid for dipping shrimp.

Lillian Ferroni Newton

MARINATED SHRIMP

INGREDIENTS:

1 pound butter (melted)
1 cup olive oil
Use following ingredients according to taste:
salt, black pepper, red pepper
Tabasco sauce, worcestershire sauce
rosemary seasoning, wine

PROCEDURE:

Mix all ingredients together. Pour over washed shrimp and marinate over night. Place shrimp in oven and cook for 15 to 20 minutes in hot oven at 375 degrees.

Josie Belleto

ITALIAN SHRIMP STEW

INGREDIENTS:

1 pound peeled deveined shrimp (if large cut in half)	
1 large onion, chopped fine	**1 large bay leaf**
¼ cup chopped shallots	**½ cup cooking oil**
2 tablespoons parsley flakes	**½ cup flour**
2 cloves garlic, minced	**1 can tomato sauce**
2 tablespoons chopped green pepper	**1 tablespoon sugar**
1 teaspoon basil	**4 cups hot water**
1 teaspoon curry powder	**2 large potatoes, peeled and diced**

PROCEDURE:

Make light brown roux with flour and oil, add onions and cook until onions are clear. Add tomato sauce, shallots, parsley, garlic, green pepper, basil, curry powder, bay leaf, sugar and water. Cook in heavy sauce pan with cover about 20 minutes. Add shrimp and potatoes and cook about 30 minutes or until potatoes are cooked. Serve over rice.

Felicia Rotolo Usner

TEMPURA BATTER

INGREDIENTS:

2 eggs
¾ cup of all purpose flour
1 cup water

1 tablespoon cornstarch
½ teaspoon salt
½ teaspoon baking powder

PROCEDURE:

Beat eggs until fluffy. Add remaining ingredients and mix. Batter is good for anything that calls for batter. (shrimp, eggplants, string beans, spinach, mushrooms, etc.) Be sure to fry in deep oil and be sure it is hot.

Aline Canalizo

CRABMEAT CONTESSA

INGREDIENTS:

1 pound cooked crab meat
4 tablespoons sour cream
salt and pepper to taste
2 shallots chopped (green parts only)

¾ ounce white wine
bread crumbs
Parmesan cheese

PROCEDURE:

Mix first 5 ingredients (crab meat, sour cream, salt and pepper, shallots and wine) Sprinkle bread crumbs and cheese on top. Place in 350 degree oven until bubbly. Serve immediately.

TORTORICI'S RESTAURANT

CRABMEAT DIP

INGREDIENTS:

1 pound crabmeat (fresh or frozen)
1 can evaporated cream
1 8-ounce jar Cheez whiz
3 tablespoons plain flour
½ cup butter

½ cup shallots (chopped fine)
¼ cup celery (chopped fine)
¼ cup parsley (fresh or flakes)
dash cayenne pepper

PROCEDURE:

Melt butter, add flour, cook over low heat until golden. Add shallots, celery and parsley to above mixture and simmer. Add cream, simmer about 10 minutes. Blend in cheese and crabmeat and season to taste with salt, pepper and cayenne pepper. Ready to serve, warm or cold.

Mrs. Rena Falcone

RED FISH COURTBOULLION

INGREDIENTS:

2 onions
2 green peppers
2 garlic toes
parsley

1 large can tomatoe sauce (16 ounces)
1 whole can tomatoes (16 ounces)
8 slices red fish

PROCEDURE:

Saute' the onions, green peppers, garlic, parsley. Add the tomato sauce and the tomatoes, cook for 30 minutes, add 8 slices red fish and cook on low fire about 15 minutes. Serve over hot rice. Salt and pepper to taste.

Beulah DeSalvo (Vince's Seafood)

FRIED COD FISH

INGREDIENTS:

Dried cod fish
1 egg
flour

milk
salt
pepper

PROCEDURE:

Cut dried cod fish into serving pieces. Soak in cool water about 8 hours — depending on amount of salt in fish. Strain and rinse in cool water. Mix egg and milk together for batter. Season batter to taste. Dip fish in batter. Roll in flour. Fry in deep fat until golden brown.

Rosie Zito

BREAST OF CHICKEN XAVIER
(Created by Chef Nick Mosca)

INGREDIENTS:

2 boneless chicken breasts (quartered)	1 teaspoon accent
4 ounces sliced mushrooms	2 tablespoons Lea and Perrin
16 oysters chopped	juice of one freshly squeezed lemon
8 artichoke bottoms	1 clove of garlic, crushed
12 thin slices Prosciutto ham	4 ounces butter
2 teaspoons chopped parsley	4 ounces Chablis wine

equal amounts of flour and seasoned bread crumbs

PROCEDURE:

Salt and pepper chicken and sprinkle with mixture of flour and seasoned bread crumbs. Melt butter in skillet and saute' garlic, mushrooms and parsley for two to three minutes, add chicken pieces and prosciutto ham and saute' for five minutes. Add lemon juice, Lea and Perrin, accent, artichoke bottoms and wine. Let simmer until chicken has cooked through and sauce begins to thicken. Divide into equal portions and serve.

Chef Nick Mosca
Elmwood Plantation

CHICKEN CACCIATORE

INGREDIENTS:

2 2½ to 3 pound fryers cut up
1 medium onion, cut up fine
½ medium to large green pepper,
    cut fine
2 cloves garlic, minced
½ teaspoon salt
¼ teaspoon black pepper
½ teaspoon oregano
½ teaspoon allspice

1 No. 2½ can tomatoes
    (crushed including juice)
1 8-ounce can tomato sauce
½ cup dry white or red wine
1 bay leaf
½ teaspoon thyme
½ teaspoon celery seed
dash of cayenne
1 cup chicken bouillon

PROCEDURE:

Brown chicken in electric frying pan or any large pan, preferably teflon, but not neccesary. Add the cup of bouillon. Add onions and green pepper. Simmer about 5 minutes, add remaining ingredients. Simmer, uncovered 30 to 40 minutes or until chicken is tender. Stir occasionally. If sauce thickens too rapidly, add about 1 cup of water. When chicken is done and sauce is thick, serve immediately with a side dish of cooked linguini al dente . Spoon sauce over linguini, use Romano or Parmesan cheese. Spaghetti may also be used if linguini is unavailable. Linguini is a flat thin spaghetti-like noodle. Add a tossed salad and fresh fruit for dessert.

Mae Bingo

GLAZED FRUITED CHICKEN

INGREDIENTS:

1 jar (29 ounces) fruits for salad
⅔ cup mayonnaise
1 package (7 ounce) herb stuffing
1 jar (12 ounce) orange marmalade

1 broiler fryer chicken, cut in parts
½ teaspoon salt
dash of pepper

PROCEDURE:

Drain fruit, set aside. Reserve ⅔ cup liquid. Stir reserved liquid into mayonnaise. Stir constantly over medium heat until mixture boils. Add stuffing. Spread in 13 x 9 x 2 inch pan. Add chicken. Sprinkle salt and pepper; brush with additional mayonnaise. Bake in oven at 350 degrees. Melt marmalade. Arrange fruit around chicken. Brush on marmalade. Bake 15 minutes. Garnish with parsley. Serves 4.

Rose Mary Vicari

BAKED CHICKEN PARMESAN

INGREDIENTS:

2 fryer chickens, cut up
1 cup chicken bouillon
4 tablespoons grated Parmesan cheese

1 cup fresh sliced mushrooms
or 2 to 4 ounce cans mushrooms

PROCEDURE:

Mix together: 1 tablespoon oregano, 1 teaspoon salt, ½ teaspoon paprika, ½ teaspoon garlic powder. Season chicken with above ingredients. Place chicken in uncovered pan (spray pan with pam to prevent sticking or use teflon lined pan) Place in oven for 30 minutes, at 350 to 375 degrees. Turn chicken and add bouillon. Cover pan, cook another 20 minutes. Add mushrooms and sprinkle chicken evenly with cheese. Bake uncovered another 15 minutes or until tender, brown and crispy. Serve with Italian baked potatoes and a tossed salad.

Mae Bingo

MINTED CHICKEN

INGREDIENTS:

1 chicken, cut up
3 tablespoons oil
1 onion, finely chopped
2 cloves garlic, chopped
1 small can mushrooms, drained

3 tablespoons flour
1 can chicken broth
3 tablespoons white wine
3 tablespoons chopped mint
   (fresh, if available)

PROCEDURE:

Brown chicken in oil until golden. Place in 9" x 14" casserole (approximate size, so chicken will be in a single layer) that is oven proof. Saute' onion and garlic until onion is clear and lightly golden. Add mushrooms. Add flour and cook until it is light brown. Stir in chicken broth, wine, and mint. Pour liquid over chicken. Salt and pepper. Bake covered at 350 degrees for 35 minutes. Aluminum foil covering works fine. Serve with rice or noodles.

Wanda Francipane

CHICKEN LORENZO

INGREDIENTS:

3 pound chicken cut and skinned
3 tablespoons olive oil
1 medium onion, sliced
2 ribs celery sliced including leaves
3 cloves garlic, minced
2 bay leaves

½ cup white vermouth
salt, pepper, paprika, thyme
and Italian seasoning
1 tablespoon flour
1 brown in bag

For Sauce:

¼ cup apple cider vinegar
¼ cup water
½ cup chili sauce
1 teaspoon mustard

2 tablespoons Lea and Perrin sauce
¼ teaspoon salt
½ teaspoon sugar
3 dashes tabasco

PROCEDURE:

Preheat oven to 350 degrees. Brush chicken parts with olive oil. Salt and pepper, sprinkle top with paprika, thyme and Italian seasoning. Add one tablespoon of flour to Brown in Bag. Coat all sides. Place Brown in Bag in large shallow pan. Place onion slices (separate in rings) and celery in bottom of bag. Place chicken on vegetables. Add bay leaves and minced garlic. Pour half cup vermouth over chicken and around the bag. Close bag with twist tie and puncture six holes on top. Place pan in oven, bake one hour. While chicken is cooking, make the sauce.

In a small saucepan, combine all sauce ingredients. Simmer about 15 minutes. Set aside.

Remove chicken from oven; let cool to handle. Make a small slit on top of bag to remove chicken. Gently remove bones from breast and legs. Place chicken in a casserole. Combine liquid and vegetables from the bag with the sauce, simmer a few minutes. Pour sauce over chicken, bake half hour uncovered in a 350 degree oven.

Marie Toscano

CHICKEN TETRAZZINI

INGREDIENTS:

1 fryer, boiled
3 stalks celery

1 onion
salt and pepper

Boil onion and celery in with chicken. Take chicken off bone.

1 medium jar pimento
1 can cream of chicken soup
cheese, grated (Cheddar)

1 package (12 ounce) elbow macaroni
(cooked)
1 can cream of mushroom soup

PROCEDURE:

Mix chicken, macaroni and all ingredients in ½ cup broth and spread cheese on top. Bake about 20 minutes or until cheese is melted.

Anna Mae Saluto St. Pierre

POLLO LIMONE ALLA ZIA GRACIA

INGREDIENTS:

1 4-pound frying chicken, cut up	1 teaspoon paprika
juice of a large lemon	2 cloves garlic (minced)
¼ cup olive oil	1 small onion (minced)
1 teaspoon oregano	salt and pepper to taste

PROCEDURE:

Mix all ingredients except chicken in large bowl. Place chicken pieces in bowl and marinate overnight in refrigerator. Broil chicken at 450 degrees 20 minutes on each side. Basting often with marinate liquid.

Grace Panepinto

GRACE'S BAKED CHICKEN

INGREDIENTS:

1 fryer, cut up	½ teaspoon garlic salt
salt and pepper	1 tablespoon oregano
1 cup vegetable oil	¼ cup grated Parmesan cheese
3 cups seasoned bread crumbs	

PROCEDURE:

Dip chicken in oil. Mix bread crumbs, garlic, oregano and grated Parmesan cheese. Roll chicken in mixture and lay on a shallow baking pan. Do not turn. Sprinkle again with Parmesan cheese and bake in 350 degree oven for one hour.

Grace Panepinto

Meats

SALTIMBOCCA ALLA ROMANA
(Roman Veal Medallions)

INGREDIENTS:

8 very thin slices of veal, each about 4 by 5 inches
½ teaspoon sage   ¼ pound butter
8 slices prosciutto   pepper to taste

PROCEDURE:

Sprinkle each slice of veal with pepper and sage. (Do not use salt, because the true Italian type prosciutto is already salted). Secure with toothpick 1 thin slice of prosciutto on each slice of veal (or you may use skewer). Saute' each slice gently in butter for 5 to 6 minutes on each side. (This recipe can be ideally prepared in a chafing dish).

Colette Bosco

AUNT THERESA'S SALTIMBOCCA

INGREDIENTS:

12 pieces veal cutlets, sliced thin   12 slices ham to cover veal cutlets
    and square   12 slices Romano cheese (can be
1 cup plain bread crumbs   sliced if at room temperature)
¼ cup chopped parsley   butter
¼ cup grated Romano cheese
olive oil

PROCEDURE:

1). Tenderize by beating.
2). Brown plain bread crumbs in frying pan. Use no oil or butter of any kind. Keep stirring crumbs so they won't burn.

55

3). Add chopped parsley, grated Romano cheese and add enough olive oil to bread crumbs until mixture sticks together.

4). Coat veal on one side in bread crumb mixture, put a slice of ham and a slice of cheese on each. Fold cutlet in half and put in baking dish. Dot generously with butter. Bake in 375 degree oven until browned, about an hour. Add water if it looks too brown during baking.

Virginia Amato

SALTIMBOCCA (Veal Roman Style)

INGREDIENTS:

2 pounds veal cutlets
½ pound prosciutto (imported Italian ham) or domestic boiled ham
¾ pound Mozzarella cheese   **1 small thinly sliced onion**
¼ cup olive oil   **salt and pepper to taste**
1 tablespoon butter   **½ cup dry white wine**

PROCEDURE:

In frying pan, melt butter and add olive oil. Quickly brown the veal cutlets and remove. Add onion, salt and pepper to same pan and saute' until turning brown. Be careful not to burn. Then add wine and bring to a boil. Lower heat and stir, and simmer for 5 minutes.

In large oven pan, which has been lightly greased with butter, place the lightly browned veal cutlets, making sure each cutlet touches the bottom of the pan. Place a slice of ham on each cutlet topped with a thin slice of cheese. Pour wine sauce over the contents of the pan, and place in 350 degree oven for 15 minutes or until cheese is melted and begins to brown slightly. Serve with boiled rice for a Roman feast.

Antoinette Maselli

MAMA CELIA'S ROLLED VEAL

INGREDIENTS:

2 cups Italian style bread crumbs   **1 lemon**
1 cup grated Romano cheese   **1 tablespoon oregano**
3 cloves garlic, finely chopped   **⅓ cup olive oil**
2 tablespoons chopped parsley   **salt and pepper to taste**
8 veal cutlets, sliced VERY thin (I get the butcher to slice them on slicing machine)

PROCEDURE:

Mix all ingredients except veal and lemon. Cut veal into 2 inch pieces. Dip into crumb mixture. Roll veal and secure with toothpick. While rolling, stuff with additional crumb mixture. Individual skewers may be used and three or four rolls put on each one. Bake in 350 degree oven about 20 minutes, until edges brown. After baking, drizzle with juice of lemon. Serve hot, with lemon wedge. Yields 25 rolls. Serves 4 to 6 for dinner. These rolls may be cut in half, before baking, and used as an hors d'oeuvre. Great with potato salad.

Grandmother prepared this dish for us as a special treat.

Bette Montaldo

THOMASSINA'S VEAL SCALLOPINE MARSALA

INGREDIENTS:

8 slices veal cutlets
1 pound fresh mushrooms
1 cup Marsala wine (domestic)
   or Sauterne wine

1 tablespoons lemon juice
flour mixed with salt and pepper
2 slices lemon

PROCEDURE:

Flour veal slices on both sides and lay aside. Slice mushrooms and saute' in butter or margarine, remove from pan. Using same pan, quickly brown veal slices on both sides and remove from pan. Add Marsala wine to pan bring to a fast boil, then lower heat. Add veal slices, turn them and the gravy will thicken. Add mushrooms. You may have to add a little water and wine if gravy is too thick. Add the lemon juice and then add two thin slices of fresh lemon on top of veal, cover and simmer for about 30 to 45 minutes.

I have served fresh zucchini sauted in tomato sauce with this or over cooked rice.

½ teaspoon sugar
4 ounces or ½ can tomato sauce
½ teaspoon granulated garlic
4 small zucchini (salt to taste)
1 tablespoon cooking oil

Cut zucchini in half and then in slices, saute' them in pan with oil, salt and garlic. When tender add tomato sauce and sugar. Let simmer for about 20 minutes.

Rosie Scanio Thomassie

VEAL SCALLOPINI

INGREDIENTS:

1½ pound veal round steak
¼ cup all-purpose flour
1 teaspoon paprika
1 3-ounce can broiled,
   sliced mushrooms
1 teaspoon beef-flavored gravy base

½ cup tomato sauce
2 tablespoons chopped
   green peppers
4 ounces medium noodles
Parmesan cheese

PROCEDURE:

Pound meat thoroughly with meat mallet. Cut into serving pieces, coat with flour seasoned with ½ teaspoon salt, dash pepper, and paprika. Brown in a little hot shortening, put in 9x9x2 inch baking dish. Drain mushrooms, reserving liquid, add water to mushroom liquid, to make ½ cup, heat to boiling. Stir in beef-flavored gravy base and pour over meat.

Bake covered at 350 degrees for 30 minutes, combining tomato sauce, green peppers, and mushrooms. Pour over meat and bake uncovered for 15 minutes. Meanwhile, cook noodles until tender, in large amount boiling water. Add salt. Drain, and baste meat with sauce just before serving. Sprinkle with Parmesan cheese. Serve with hot buttered noodles.

Mrs. Helen Chimento

VEAL SCALOPPINE MARSALA

INGREDIENTS:

8 thin slices veal cutlets
¾ cup cooking oil
1 cup Marsala wine

1½ sticks pure butter
salt and pepper

PROCEDURE:

Cut around edge of veal so it will not curl when cooking. Cut into individual pieces and pound. Salt and pepper well on each side then dip into flour and lay on paper towels.

Put cooking oil in large skillet, and when oil begins to bubble, fry veal for ONLY A FEW SECONDS on each side. Remove and put aside.

In another large skillet slowly melt butter. Put flame on simmer and when butter is hot, add veal and gently pour wine over veal a little at a time. Simmer until piping hot and serve immediately -- OR -- as veal is taken from simmering mixture it can be placed in a baking dish and placed in the oven. If left in oven for a few minutes cover with foil until ready to serve.

Goffredo Fraccaro
Chef-Owner, LaRiviera Ristorante

VEAL POCKET
(7 - 10 pounds -- cut off shoulder)

INGREDIENTS:

3 cups bread cubes
4 dozen oysters (clean oysters, reserve, and strain liquid)
1 cup celery
1 cup green onions
1 small onion
3 cloves garlic
¼ cup parsley
1 cup Italian cheese

1½ sticks butter
¼ teaspoon thyme
Kitchen bouquet
2 slices bacon
¼ cup olive oil
1 8-ounce can mushrooms

PROCEDURE:

Rub inside of pocket with salt and pepper. Saute' green onions and the small onion in ¼ cup olive oil and ½ stick butter. When wilted, add oysters and simmer until oyster edges curl. Salt and pepper to taste. Add finely chopped garlic and parsley. Add oyster liquid. (Note: If more liquid is needed, you may add water to oyster liquid.) Simmer 2 or 3 minutes and remove from heat.

Drain and saute' mushrooms in ½ stick butter. Set aside. Combine bread cubes, Italian cheese, celery, thyme, and add sauteed mushrooms. Add this to oyster liquid mixture and toss lightly. Salt and pepper to taste. Do not stir mixture, as it will produce a sticky consistency as opposed to the desired light and fluffy mixture. Stuff into veal pocket, close with skewers. Brush entire pocket with Kitchen Bouquet. Place 2 strips of bacon on pocket and bake on rack in 350 degree oven for at least 3 or 3½ hours, according to size of pocket. Remove pocket from oven. Let it set a while before slicing in ½ inch slices.

Vivian Castelluccio

OSSI BUCHI ALLA GENOVESE
(Genoa Style)

INGREDIENTS:

6 pieces marrow bone (medium size with meat attached)
2 medium carrots
2 medium onions
2 stalks celery
3 large cloves garlic
⅔ cup olive oil
⅓ cup olive oil
1 can (16 ounce) Imported Italian plum tomatoes with basilico

1 heaping teaspoon nutmeg
½ pound frozen green peas
½ cup imported pine nuts
1 cup golden seedless raisins
1 cup white dry sherry

PROCEDURE:

Wash meat, towel dry, salt and pepper well on both sides. Put aside on paper towels. Take carrots, onions, celery, and ⅔ cup olive oil and add to food processor and blend to a consistency so fine it is almost mush. If you do not have a food processor, chop extremely fine and blend with ⅔ cup olive oil.

In large pot, add ⅓ cup olive oil and braise cloves of garlic. Pound each clove once before braising. After braising well, remove and throw away garlic. Add vegetable mixture to the pot and begin cooking on medium heat still stirring frequently. Put Italian tomatoes in food processor and puree. Add nutmeg to mixture which is cooking. Stir, add tomatoes to cooking mixture and turn fire low. Add salt to taste, let mixture simmer still stirring. Take peas, raisins, pine nuts, and soak in warm water for a few minutes. Return to meat which was put aside and flour on both sides. In separate skillet put ¾ cup cooking oil and when oil begins to bubble, brown meat on both sides. When lightly browned, remove and line in baking pan.

At this point, add dry white sherry to cooking mixture. Stir.

Strain peas, raisins and pine nuts and add to cooking mixture. Mixture should have been cooking for approximately 20 minutes. Let this entire mixture simmer for another 5 minutes and pour over meat lined in baking pan. Cover with foil and bake for 1 hour at 375 degrees. Can be served with white rice.

Goffredo Fraccaro
Chef-Owner, La Riviera Ristorante

LEG OF LAMB ROAST

INGREDIENTS:

Leg of lamb roast	flour
3 buds of garlic	1 medium onion (chopped fine)
salt and pepper to taste	2 tablespoon parsley

PROCEDURE:

Cut narrow gashes in meat and place slivers of garlic in them. Season with salt and pepper and dredge with flour. Place on rack in 325 degree oven and roast 30-45 minutes per pound. Do not baste or cover. When done, remove from pan and keep warm while making gravy.

GRAVY — Pour off all but 3 tablespoons fat from pan drippings and add 2 tablespoons flour. Blend and stir til golden brown. Add to this one finely chopped medium sized onion and saute' until wilted. Add 1 to 2 cups boiling water and stir until blended. Season with salt and pepper and 2 tablespoons finely chopped parsley. Serve with rice or boiled new potatoes.

Gene Elmer

SHISHKABOBS ITALIANA

INGREDIENTS:

½ teaspoon crushed oregano
½ cup Italian salad dressing
¼ cup lemon juice
¼ teaspoon garlic powder
Hot cooked rice

¼ teaspoon of salt
1/8 teaspoon of pepper
2 pounds boneless lamb
   cut into 2 inch squares

PROCEDURE:

Combine salad dressing, lemon juice, oregano, garlic powder and meat. Cover and marinate 2 hours at room temperature or overnight in refrigerator, turning meat several times. Remove meat from marinated sauce and place on skewers. Season with salt to taste. Grill 25 minutes over medium heat, basting with marinated sauce and turning occasionally. Serve over rice. Serves 4 people.

Joyce Kass

ROGNONCINI TRIFOLATI
(Sauteed Sliced Kidneys)

INGREDIENTS:

8 veal kidneys
2 tablespoons butter
4 tablespoons olive oil
2 teaspoons finely chopped garlic
2 tablespoons finely chopped fresh parsley
   (Italian type if possible)

2 tablespoons lemon juice
salt to taste
freshly ground black pepper

PROCEDURE:

NOTE: Boiling of the kidneys is for filtration. Add a pinch of baking soda. This will keep down odor as well as cleansing. Boil for approximately 30 minutes. Drain well. Cook.

With a small sharp knife peel off the thin membrane that covers each kidney and cut away the knob of fat under it. Then cut the kidneys crosswise into paper-thin slices. In a heavy skillet, melt the butter with the olive oil. As soon as the foam subsides, toss in the kidneys and cook them over moderately high heat, stirring and turning the slices constantly, for 2 minutes approximately. Then add the garlic and parsley and cook, stirring constantly, for another 1 or 2 minutes or until kidneys are lightly browned. Pour in the lemon juice and let it boil up once, then turn off the heat. Taste the sauce and season it with salt and pepper. Serve immediately. Serves 4.

Sue Dandry

FRESH KIDNEY STEW WITH PASTA

INGREDIENTS:

Fresh kidneys (2 - 3) depending on size
  (if small) VEAL ONLY
2 tablespoons plain flour
1 large onion

1 celery heart
2 green onions (Shallot) and
  fresh parsley
black pepper and salt

PROCEDURE:

Cut up bite size pieces being sure to cut away gristle and white fat from kidneys. Wash fresh kidneys thoroughly. Fry two (2) tablespoons of flour along with a large onion making a dark roux. Add fresh kidneys, freshly cut parsley and one celery heart chopped along with (shallot) green onions chopped, black pepper and salt to taste. Cover kidneys about 2'' above with hot water, adding additional hot water if and when needed while cooking. Slowly cook kidneys on a low fire for 2 or 2½ hours or until kidneys are tender.

Boil a pound of spaghetti. (thin spaghetti preferred) Over hot spaghetti spoon the freshly cooked kidney stew.

Lillian Guichard

SALSICCIA CON PEPERONI

INGREDIENTS:

1½ pounds Italian sausage with anise
4 green peppers (quartered) (take seeds out)

salt to taste
½ cup water

PROCEDURE:

Put cold sausage in frying pan with ½ cup water for 20 minutes. After water evaporates and sausage is brown, turn and brown on the other side the same way. Add green pepper. If dry add a little oil. Cook until peppers are done.

CAMP SEA BEAN BRUNCH

INGREDIENTS:

8 slices bread (crust off)
2 large white onions, chopped fine
1 can sliced mushrooms
2 pounds smoked sausage, sliced fine
2 pounds yellow cheese, grated
8 eggs, beaten

1 cup milk
1 cup Parmesan cheese
1 teaspoon Tabasco sauce
1 teaspoon oregano
1 teaspoon salt
1 teaspoon pepper

PROCEDURE:

Line deep tin biscuit pan with foil. Place bread in bottom of pan. Sprinkle chopped onions over bread. Sprinkle grated cheese over onions. Sprinkle mushrooms over cheese. Place sausage in layer over mushrooms. Combine eggs and milk, beat and pour over layered mixture. Sprinkle Tabasco sauce, salt, pepper and oregano over top. Cover with heavy layer of Parmesan cheese. Bake in oven thirty minutes at 350 degrees; then broil for approximately ten minutes. Serves eight.

NOTE: This casserole can be prepared the night before and kept in refrigerator until ready to bake.

Voris King

ITALIAN GRAVY WITH ROAST-ITALIAN SAUSAGE AND MEAT BALLS

INGREDIENTS:

¼ cup cooking oil
6 (6 ounce) cans tomato paste
1 (16 ounce) can whole tomatoes
3 onions (medium size) chopped
1 small to medium garlic head, chopped

2 tablespoons sugar
4 or 5 bay leaves
salt and pepper to taste

PROCEDURE:

Fry onions in oil until soft, not brown, add garlic continue frying about two minutes. Cut up whole tomatoes add to the above, cook about 10 minutes, add tomatoe paste and cook another 10 minutes stirring constantly, add about 4 quarts of water and bay leaves. Cook about 2½ to 3 hours. While this is cooking prepare roast and Italian sausage.

1 - 2 or 3 pounds roast (beef or pork) Small pieces of Italian cheese and garlic toes.

Stuff roast with cheese and garlic toes, fry until brown on all sides, add to gravy.

Italian sausage - fry in a little oil about 5 minutes, add to gravy.

Italian Meat Balls

2 pounds ground meat
1 cup bread crumbs
½ cup Italian cheese, grated
2 tablespoons chopped parsley
1 medium size onion chopped

8 toes of garlic chopped
4 or 5 eggs
2 tablespoons chopped mint
salt and pepper to taste

63

PROCEDURE:

Combine all above ingredients, mix well, make into balls (size desired). Fry or bake a few minutes until a little brown, add to gravy. Continue cooking gravy stirring occasionally until done, Serve over hot spaghetti.

Mrs. Frank Damico

STUFFED BEEF ROLL
(Stuffed Rolled Steak)

INGREDIENTS:

1 large baby beef round steak
2 hard boiled eggs
1 cup Italian bread crumbs
1 onion (chopped fine)
1 celery stalk (chopped fine)
¼ bell pepper (chopped fine)

2 - 3 toes garlic (chopped fine)
¼ cup Parmesan cheese (grated)
olive oil
salt and pepper
heavy thread

PROCEDURE:

Salt and pepper steak and lay flat. Mix bread crumbs, onions, celery, bell peppers, garlic, Parmesan cheese. Moisten with a little olive oil an and spread over steak. Place eggs at one end and roll as you would a jelly roll. Secure with toothpicks until tied. Wrap and tie securely with thread. Brown rolled steak in a little oil on all sides then drop into prepared red gravy. Simmer for 1½ to 2½ hours or until tender.

RED GRAVY

1 pound Italian sausage (optional) sliced in small pieces
2 cans tomato paste
2 cans tomato sauce
1 tablespoon sugar
1 large onion (chopped)
1 whole garlic (can be chopped or used whole)

1 celery stalk (chopped)
½ bell pepper (chopped)
1 tablespoon parsley flakes
olive oil
2 bay leaves

PROCEDURE:

Fry Italian sausage in a little oil until done. Saute' onions, garlic, celery, bell peppers, parsley until tender. Simmer tomato **paste** in drippings. Stir in sugar. Add tomato sauce stirring constantly so it doesn't burn. Fill empty cans with warm water and stir into gravy. Add sausage and seasonings. Simmer for about ½ hour before adding beef roll.

To serve, cut thread off roll and slice ½ inch thick pieces. Each piece should have an inner circle of egg surrounded by bread crumb stuffing encircled by meat. Serve with spaghetti or noodles.

Sandi Ricks

TEXAS BARBEQUE BRISKET

INGREDIENTS:

1 beef brisket, 5 - 7 pounds
1 cup catsup
1 cup beer (optional), or
    1 cup juice of meat or water
¼ cup vinegar
2 tablespoons sugar
1 teaspoon salt
1 dash liquid smoke
1 dash soy sauce
1 dash tabasco sauce
½ teaspoon Lea and Perrins sauce
salt, garlic salt, pepper to season meat

PROCEDURE:

Place brisket in baking pan, fat side up, sprinkle liberally with salt, garlic salt and pepper. Cover tightly and cook at 250 degrees for 5 hours. Remove from pan, trim fat, and discard all but one cup of juice.

SAUCE: Mix 1 cup catsup, ¼ cup vinegar, the cup of saved juice or 1 cup beer or water, and the rest of the seasonings. Simmer 30 minutes. Put meat back into baking pan, and pour sauce over it. Cover and cook 1 hour at 250 degrees. Serve sliced like roast, or on buns. Freezes well.

Jeanne Bernard

ITALIAN STUFFED PORK CHOPS

INGREDIENTS:

6 pork chops 1 inch thick with a pocket
salt and pepper the chops
2 tablespoons olive oil
½ pound ground meat
3 links Italian sausage

1 onion chopped
2 cloves of garlic chopped
a little of shallots and
parsley may be added

Saute' the above ingredients and add:

1 cup bread crumbs
4 tablespoons Italian cheese

1 egg
2 tablespoons oleo

PROCEDURE:

Salt and pepper to taste, add some water if dry. Stuff the pork chops and put a toothpick to hold it together. Put the stuffed chops in a pan with a little of water. Pour some cooking sherry wine on top and cover with foil. Bake in oven at 350 degrees for 1 hour. Then remove foil and continue baking for ½ hour at 400 degrees, basting often. You may substitute oysters or ham in the stuffings.

Genevieve Panepinto Harris

PORK CHOPS ITALIAN STYLE

INGREDIENTS:
8 thick pork chops
2 tablespoons oil
salt and pepper
1 pound elbow macaroni, cooked, drained
4 (10¾ ounce) cans condensed cream of mushroom soup
2 (10 ounce) packages chopped spinach, thawed, squeezed dry
2 cloves minced garlic
1½ cups milk or dry white wine
½ cup grated Parmesan cheese

PROCEDURE:

Season chops with salt and pepper, then brown in skillet on both sides in oil. Line two 13"x 9" x2" casseroles with foil. Mix macaroni and spinach. Spoon equal amounts of each into 2 casseroles. Place 4 chops on top of each. Mix soup, garlic, and milk or wine. Spoon equal amounts over chops in casseroles. Sprinkle with cheese. Bake in preheated oven for 1 hour at 350 degrees. Serves 8 - or freeze one casserole for later use.

BREADED MEAT WITH BEEF OR PORK

INGREDIENTS:
Cuts of meat that can be used:

1 beef or 2 veal round steaks, tenderized, cut thin
6 to 8 veal rib chops   2 eggs, beaten
6 to 8 pork chops   cooking oil

Dry mixture -
1 teaspoon onion powder
1 teaspoon garlic powder
½ cup Italian bread crumbs or more if needed
½ cup plain bread crumbs or more if needed
1 heaping tablespoon Italian cheese, grated
¼ cup parsley, chopped

PROCEDURE:

Slit meat on all sides to prevent curling while frying. Salt and pepper meat and also beaten eggs. Dip in beaten eggs, then in dry mixture.

Fry on little higher than medium heat in a generous amount of cooking oil in fry pan. Meat will stick to bottom of pan if you don't use enough oil. Brown on both sides and drain on paper towels.

Anna Whittle

COSTOLETTE di MAIALE alla PIZZAIOLA
(Braised Pork Chops with Tomato and Garlic Sauce)

INGREDIENTS:

4 tablespoons olive oil
6 center-cut loin pork chops - 1 to 1½'' thick
1 teaspoon finely chopped garlic
½ teaspoon dried oregano, crumbled
¼ teaspoon dried thyme, crumbled
½ bay leaf
½ teaspoon salt
½ cup dry red wine
1 cup drained canned tomatoes chopped fine
1 tablespoon tomato paste
½ pound green peppers, seeded and cut in 2'' strips
    (about 1¼ cups)
½ pound fresh sliced mushrooms

PROCEDURE:

In heavy skillet heat 2 tablespoons olive oil. Brown chops on each side and transfer to a plate. Pour off almost all fat then cook garlic, oregano, thyme, bay leaf and salt stirring constantly for 3 minutes. Add wine and boil briskly to reduce it to about ¼ cup. Stir in the tomatoes and tomato paste and return the chops to skillet. Baste with sauce, cover and simmer over low heat, basting once or twice for 45 minutes. Meanwhile heat the remaining oil in another large skillet. Fry the green pepper in oil for approximately 5 minutes stirring frequently. Add mushrooms and toss with pepper for a minute or two then transfer in pan with pork chops. Cover and simmer until chops are tender and sauce is thick enough to coat a spoon heavily. To serve, arrange the chops on a platter and spoon vegetables and sauce over them.

Sue Dandry

TRIPPA alla FIORENTINA
(Braised Tripe with Tomato Sauce)

INGREDIENTS:

¼ cup olive oil
¾ cup finely chopped onions

½ cup finely chopped celery
2 pounds honeycomb tripe cut into strips long and thin
3 tablespoons tomato paste
2 tablespoons finely chopped fresh parsley
½ teaspoon finely chopped garlic
½ teaspoon salt
½ cup freshly grated imported Parmesan cheese

PROCEDURE:

In a heavy 4 quart sauce pan heat olive oil. Add onion and celery and cook over medium heat for 10 minutes, stirring constantly until onions and celery are soft and slightly golden brown. Add tripe and toss with onions and celery until they are well combined. Dissolve the tomato paste with a little water and pour over tripe and vegetables. Add parsley, garlic and salt. Bring to boil over high heat, then reduce the heat, cover pan and simmer the tripe slowly, regulating the heat so that the surface of the sauce barely moves. If at any point the sauce becomes too thick, add a few tablespoons of water. In 2½ to 3 hours the tripe should be tender when pierced with fork. Serve by sprinkling each serving with grated cheese.
Serves 4.

Sue Dandry

DUCKS A LA KINGWOOD

INGREDIENTS:

2 ducks	**1/8 bell pepper**
½ stalk celery	**salt**
1 medium bunch green onions	**red pepper**
1 large white onion	**black pepper**
8 toes garlic	**flour**

PROCEDURE:

Chop very fine the celery, tops of the green onions, the white onion, garlic and bell pepper. (Altogether this seasoning should amount to approximately three cups.) Place in bottom of black iron pot.

Salt and pepper the carcasses of two ducks heavily, both inside and out. This must be rubbed into the carcasses by hand. Place the ducks in the above heavy iron dutch oven, breast up, and then sprinkle more black pepper, salt, and a slight amount of red pepper on them. Using a sieve, sprinkle the duck carcasses with flour until they are well covered. Using a pitcher, pour water into the pot gently, being careful not to wash the flour from the ducks, but completely covering the ducks with water. Place the iron lid on the dutch oven and put in oven which has been preheated to 500 degrees. Cook exactly two hours. At no time during the cooking should you remove the lid to inspect the ducks. At the end of the two hours, on removing the dutch oven, you will find the ducks beautifully browned, juicy, and a dish fit for a king. Should they not be as brown as desired, remove the lid and return to the oven for five minutes. In the bottom of the pot will be a very fine gravy which may be used with the balance of the meal.

Voris King

Salads

ITALIAN SALAD

INGREDIENTS: (Dressing)

¼ cup vinegar
¼ cup water
1 heaping tablespoon salt
1 heaping tablespoon black pepper
6-ounces olive oil or salad oil
2 tablespoons grated Italian cheese
2 cloves of garlic, squeezed (use a garlic press)

Shake all above ingredients together well and put aside.

1 or 2 heads lettuce
1 bell pepper, sliced
2 cucumbers, sliced
1 small onion, sliced
1 small jar green olives
½ pound black olives or 1 can ripe olives
1 package peperoni sausage, sliced
1 small jar heart of artichokes, cut in pieces
1 can cut green beans
2 sticks of celery, chopped in hunks
½ cup Italian cheese cut in cubes

PROCEDURE:

Mix together, pour dressing in and toss. If you make a small amount of salad, some of the dressing will be leftover. Keep for later use.

Anna Mae Saluto St. Pierre

70

TOSSED SALAD

INGREDIENTS:

lettuce
cucumbers
tomato slices
scallions or sliced onion
radishes
salt and pepper to taste
1 teaspoon oregano

1 teaspoon parsley flakes
½ teaspoon basil flakes
¼ teaspoon nutmeg
½ teaspoon garlic powder
½ teaspoon onion powder
oil and vinegar to taste (wine vinegar)

PROCEDURE:

To tossed salad (lettuce, cucumbers, tomato slices, scallions or sliced onion, radishes), add salt and pepper to taste. Add oregano, parsley flakes, basil flakes, nutmeg, garlic powder and onion powder. Toss together with enough oil and vinegar to taste. Use a good oil and a wine vinegar. (My "secret" ingredient is the nutmeg which gives a "nutty" flavor).

Mae Bingo

CARROT SALAD

INGREDIENTS:

2 cans sliced carrots
1 cup sugar
1 can tomato soup
¾ cup white vinegar

½ cup vegetable oil
1 sliced onion - thin rings
1 sliced bell pepper

PROCEDURE:

Combine sugar, tomato soup, white vinegar, oil. Mix. Layer carrots, onions and pepper. Pour liquid ingredients over this. Layer vegetables and repeat second step. Refrigerate for at least a day before serving. Good for several weeks.

Pat De Martini

ITALIAN CRAB SALAD

INGREDIENTS:

1 dozen boiled crabs or 2 pounds crab meat
1 jar 12-ounce sweet pickled cauliflour
1 6-ounce jar stuffed olives
1 8-ounce jar black olives
1 large head garlic

½ stalk celery
½ cup white vinegar
1 cup of pure olive oil
salt and pepper to taste

PROCEDURE:

Using boiled crabs, break in half and put in a large pan. Take all of the ingredients and cut them up and mix all together with the crabs and put in the refrigerator. Stir ever so often so it can marinate. Serve in about 4 hours or longer.

Rita Phillip

Cakes

CASSATA ALLA SICILIANA

INGREDIENTS:

1 10-inch angel food cake
1 or 2 pounds Ricotta cheese
6 - 8 table·spoons rum
½ cup confectioners sugar
½ teaspoon cinnamon

½ cup toasted chopped almonds
¼ cup chopped candied cherries
¼ cup grated semi-sweet chocolate
½ pint whipping cream

PROCEDURE:

With a serrated knife, slice cake into 4 layers, placing each layer on a separate plate except bottom layer. Place this layer on a cake plate. Sprinkle each layer with 2 tablespoons of rum. Set aside while preparing filling.

FILLING:

Beat ricotta with electric mixer until smooth. Beat in confectioners sugar. Continue to beat 3 minutes to dissolve sugar. Divide into 3 equal portions. Add chocolate to one portion and mix well; add cinnamon and nuts to second portion and mix well; add cherries to third portion and mix well. Spread bottom layer of cake with chocolate mixture; top with cake layer. Spread cinnamon and nut mixture on cake; top with third cake layer. Spread cherry portion on cake layer. Top with top cake layer.

Whip cream in chilled bowl. Add about 3 -4 teaspoonsful of sugar gradually while beating. Frost cake with whipped cream. Refrigerate immediately. Serve in one inch wedges. Serves 12 - 16.

NOTE: For a more festive occasion, add a few drops red or green food coloring to whipped cream while whipping. Decorate with a few sliced or quartered candied cherries.

Mae Bingo

MARGIE'S PINA COLADA CAKE

INGREDIENTS:
⅓ cup dark rum
1 package coconut cream flavor instant pudding
1 package white cake mix
4 eggs , ½ cup water
¼ cup oil
½ cup coconut

FROSTING INGREDIENTS:
8 ounces crushed pineapple in juice
1 package coconut cream flavor instant pudding
⅓ cup dark rum
1 9-ounce frozen whipped cream topping

PROCEDURE:
Blend all ingredients except coconut in large mixer bowl. Beat 4 minutes at medium speed of electric mixer. Add coconut. Pour into 2 greased and floured 9-inch layer pans. Bake at 350 degrees for 25 to 30 minutes or until cake springs back when lightly pressed. Do not underbake. Cool in pan 15 minutes; remove and cool on racks. Fill and frost. Sprinkle with coconut. Chill, refrigerate leftover cake.

PINA COLADA FROSTING:
Combine 1 can (8 ounce) crushed pineapple in juice, one package coconut cream flavor instant pudding and ⅓ cup dark rum in bowl; beat until well blended. Fold in one container (9 ounce) frozen whipped topping, thawed.

Deanna Hess Castelluccio

BANANA SPLIT CAKE

INGREDIENTS:

CRUST: 2 cups vanilla wafer crumbs - 1 stick melted butter or oleo

Mix: 1 cup confectioners sugar , 1 stick oleo or butter and 2 eggs

Layer: 5 or 6 bananas   one cup chopped pecans
1 large can crushed pineapple   cherries
frozen whipped topping

PROCEDURE: (For Crust)
Mix vanilla wafer crumbs and butter, press into large cake pan, 13 x 9 inches.

Mix: With mixer on high speed for 15 minutes, beat: 1 cup confectioners sugar, 1 stick oleo or butter, 2 eggs.

Layer: Spread mix over crust; 5 or 6 bananas, split lengthwise or in round slices; 1 large can crushed pineapple, drained; one layer whipped topping; one cup chopped pecans. Garnish with chopped cherries. Keep refrigerated.

Genevieve P. Harris

CASSATA alla SICILIANA
(Sicilian cake with chocolate frosting)

INGREDIENTS:

A fresh pound cake about 9" long and 3" wide
1 pound Ricotta cheese
2 tablespoons heavy cream (breakfast)
¼ cup sugar
3 tablespoons orange-flavored liqueur
3 tablespoons coarsely chopped mixed candied fruit
2 ounce semi sweet chocolate, coarsely chopped

PROCEDURE:

With a sharp serrated knife, slice the end crusts off the pound cake and level the top if it is rounded. Cut the cake horizontally into ½" to ¾" thick slabs. Rub the ricotta through a coarse sieve into a bowl with a wooden spoon and beat it with a electric beater until it is smooth. Beating constantly, add the cream, sugar and liqueur. With a rubber spatula, fold in the chopped candied fruit and chocolate. Center the bottom slab of the cake on a flat plate and spread it generously with the ricotta mixture. Carefully place another slab of cake on top, keeping sides and ends even, and spread with more ricotta. Repeat until all cake and filling has been used up; ending with a plain slice of cake on top. Gently press the loaf together to make as compact as possible. Do not worry if it feels wobbly, chilling firms the loaf. Refrigerate the cake for about 2 hours or until ricotta is firm.

CHOCOLATE FROSTING:

12 ounces semi-sweet chocolate pieces small
¾ cup strong black coffee
½ pound unsalted butter cut in ½" pieces and thoroughly chilled

Melt chocolate with coffee in small heavy saucepan over **low** heat, stirring constantly until chocolate is completely dissolved. Remove pan from heat and beat in chilled butter -- 1 piece at a time. Continue beating until mixture is smooth. Chill until it thickens to a spreading consistency. With a small metal spatula, spread the frosting evenly over top, sides and ends of the cassata, swirling to decorate to your taste. Cover loosely with aluminum foil and let ripen in refrigerator for at least 24 hours before serving.
Serves 8.

Sue Dandry

APPLE SAUCE CAKE

INGREDIENTS:

1¼ cups sifted flour
½ cup sugar
¼ teaspoon baking powder
1 teaspoon soda
1 teaspoon cinnamon
½ teaspoon nutmeg
1 teaspoon salt

½ cup brown sugar
½ cup shortening
1¼ cup apple sauce
1 egg
½ cup chopped nuts
½ cup raisins

PROCEDURE:

Sift flour, granulated sugar, baking powder, soda, salt and spices. Add brown sugar, shortening and apple sauce. Beat at medium speed for 2 minutes. Add egg, beat another 2 minutes. Stir in nuts and raisins. Pour batter into greased and floured 9-cup bundt pan. Bake at 350 degrees for 35 to 40 minutes or until cake has started to pull away from the pan.

Anna Mae Rotolo

RUM CAKE

CAKE
INGREDIENTS:

1 package yellow cake mix
1 package instant vanilla pudding mix
4 eggs
½ cup Wesson oil (don't substitute)
½ cup rum
½ cup water

½ cup chopped pecans

PROCEDURE:

Mix first six ingredients about 2 minutes combining well. Sprinkle pecans on bottom of greased tube or bundt pan. Pour in batter and bake in 325 degree oven until done, about 55 or 60 minutes. Remove from oven and pierce top thoroughly with tooth pick. Immediately pour glaze over top. Cool completely before removing from pan.

GLAZE
INGREDIENTS:

¾ stick oleo or butter
½ cup sugar

little less than ¼ cup water
1½ tablespoons rum

PROCEDURE:

Boil butter, sugar and water for one minute. Remove from heat and add rum. Pour over cake.

Anna Mae Rotolo

CUCUZZI CAKE

INGREDIENTS:

1 cucuzzi - peeled, seeded, diced, cooked & drain
(about three cups)

4 eggs (beaten)
1 tablespoon vanilla   1 teaspoon salt
1 stick butter (melted)   2 cups self rising flour
1 cup sugar

PROCEDURE:

Mash three cups cucuzzi, drain, put in eggs, salt, vanilla, butter, and sugar. Mix well then add flour. More or less flour may be added. Bisquick flour may be used. After flour is added, pour in buttered **2 quart** glass dish and bake until golden brown at 350 degrees for approximately 1 hour.

Antoinette Redding

DATE ROLL

INGREDIENTS:

1 pound dates   3 cups of pecans
1 can pet milk   ½ block butter
3½ cups sugar   2 tablespoons vanilla

PROCEDURE:

Mix sugar and pet milk, cook until it boils. Add dates and let it boil again, add nuts, butter and vanilla, cook until it forms a soft ball in water. Beat well and until cool enough to roll on damp cloth. Cover and let set in damp cloth for 2 or 3 hours then transfer to aluminum foil.

Anna Mae Saluto St. Pierre

APPLE COBBLER

INGREDIENTS:

1 stick butter   2 teaspoons baking powder
1 cup sugar   ¾ cup milk
1 cup flour   can apple pie filling

PROCEDURE:

Melt butter in 8 or 9 inch dish. Mix sugar, flour, baking powder and milk. Pour over melted butter, DO NOT STIR. Pour pie filling over mix and bake at 350 degrees for 50 minutes.

Anna Mae Rotolo

DATE SWIRLS

INGREDIENTS:

Filling:
½ pound pitted dates
⅓ cup water

¼ cup sugar
¼ cup chopped nuts

Dough Ingredients:

½ cup butter
½ cup brown sugar
½ cup white sugar
1 egg

2 cups flour
½ teaspoon soda
¼ teaspoon salt

PROCEDURE:

Cream butter, add sugar. Cream well. Add egg and beat until well mixed. Toss on lightly floured board and knead until smooth. Roll about ¼ inch thick. Spread date mixture on dough and roll like jelly roll. Wrap in wax paper and place in refrigerator overnight. Slice and bake on a greased baking sheet at 400 degrees for 10 minutes.

FILLING PROCEDURE:
Cut dates, add sugar and water. Cook for 5 minutes, stirring constantly. Add nuts. Makes 5 dozen.

Johnnie Ditcharo

PECAN STICKS

INGREDIENTS:

1 cup shortening
1 cup sugar
1 egg yolk
2 teaspoons cinnamon

2½ cups cake flour
1 tablespoon sugar
1 egg white beaten stiff
1 cup chopped pecans

PROCEDURE:

Cream shortening and 1 cup sugar together, add egg yolk, cinnamon and flour. Mix well. Spread ¼ inch thick in a well greased 10x15 inch pan. Add sugar to beaten egg whites and brush over dough. Cover with thick layer of pecans and press into dough. Bake 20 minutes at 350 degrees. Makes 75 - ½ inch sticks.

Marion Giardina

HOME MADE ITALIAN FIG COOKIES

INGREDIENTS:

6 pounds flour
11 teaspoons baking powder
10 eggs
2 pounds lard

2 pounds sugar
1 cup milk
1½ or 2 teaspoons vanilla
pinch of salt

FILLING INGREDIENTS:
2½ pounds dried ground figs
1 pound raisins

1 pound chopped walnuts
1 pint honey

PROCEDURE:

Put sugar and milk in pot and heat to less than lukewarm. Mix in beaten eggs and flour, salt, baking powder, lard, vanilla. Mix well until it forms a dough. Take small pieces of dough and roll flat into long rows. Place fig filling in center of rows and roll dough around about the size of your finger enclosing the filling. Cut rows into desired lengths. Slice edges of each length 2 - 3 times. Decorate as desired.
PROCEDURE FOR FILLING:

Ground and mix all ingredients well. Fill dough. Cut into desired shapes. Bake at 325 degrees until very light brown.

This is an authentic recipe which has been handed down through the years. There have been many variations of the original, such as adding wine, brandy, anise, etc., but the basic recipe is very good as it is. This recipe makes a large quantity. Extra dough can be used to make regular cookies by rolling dough and cutting into different designs and shapes and decorating with nuts, colored sugar, candied fruits, etc.

Gertrude Bondi

ITALIAN FIG COOKIES
(Cucurdates)

INGREDIENTS: Filling

1 pound figs
½ pound dates, pitted
½ orange skin
1 cup glaze fruit mix
¼ teaspoon black pepper
1½ teaspoon ground cinnamon

½ cup brandy or whiskey
½ cup raisins
(1 cup sugar and ½ cup water -
mix together until sugar
is melted and add to figs)

Dough

4¼ cups flour
½ cup sugar
1 teaspoon baking powder

¼ teaspoon salt
1¼ cups shortening (vegetable or butter)
½ cup plus 4 to 7 tablespoons cold water

PROCEDURE:

Sift the flour, sugar, baking powder and salt into a large bowl. Add shortening and cut in with knife or pastry blender until texture is a coarse meal. Sprinkle with a fork the water and toss lightly with fork to mix. Add remaining water, a tablespoon at a time, tossing the mix until dough will be firm and smooth. Heat oven to 275 degrees and take half the dough on a lightly floured surface, roll it out in 12x18 inch rectangles about 1/8" thick. Cut into 3" wide strips and spread 3½ to 4 tablespoons of fig filling down the center of each strip, leaving about one inch on each side. Moisten side of strips with water, fold over and press lightly with fork to seal. Cut each strip into six 2 inch cookies, cut and slit in the fold side of each cookie. Place on ungreased baking sheet, bending each cookie into a slight curve. Bake about 20 minutes until bottoms are brown. Remove from oven and cool on wire rack before icing. Repeat with remaining dough and filling.

ICING
Mix sugar, anise extract and milk. Spoon over the top of cookies. Icing may be omitted.

Grace Panepinto

ITALIAN FIG FILLED COOKIES
(PUCCIDATI)

INGREDIENTS: DOUGH

½ pound shortening
1 cup sugar
3 eggs
3½ teaspoons baking powder
4 - 6 cups flour

½ teaspoon anise flavoring
1 tablespoon vanilla
1 cup milk
¼ teaspoon salt

80

FILLING:

1 pound figs, ground up
1 pound raisins
½ pound candied fruit
skin of one orange
1 pound dates
½ pound walnuts
1 small glass grape jelly

½ cup honey
1 cup strong coffee
1 teaspoon cinnamon
1 teaspoon allspice
1 teaspoon nutmeg
½ teaspoon cloves

PROCEDURE:

Sift flour. Measure and resift with sugar, baking powder, and salt. Cut in shortening. Make a well and break eggs into it. Add half of milk and mix. Add flavorings. Knead well for about 5 minutes. Add remaining milk as you knead. Add only enough milk to make a medium soft dough and easy to handle. Divide into 3 parts. Roll into 1/8 inch thick rectangles. Place filling about 1 inch from edge. Roll dough over it. Seal by brushing with milk. When rolled, cut into shape. Place on cookie sheet and bake 8 - 10 minutes at 375 degrees.

FILLING:

Grind together 1 pound figs, 1 pound raisins, ½ pound candied fruit, skin of one orange and one pound dates, and ½ pound walnuts. Place in 2 quart saucepan. Add grape jelly, honey, coffee, cinnamon, allspice, nutmeg and cloves. Warm thoroughly, stir frequently. Fill cookie dough.

Dough can also be used for anise cookies. Just roll dough about ½ inch thick. Flatten down and bake 8 - 10 minutes. Take out and slice slantwise and bake until golden brown.

Mae Bingo

FIG COOKIES

INGREDIENTS:

COOKIE DOUGH
2 pounds flour
1½ cups sugar
¾ pound shortening
¾ teaspoon salt
Sauterne white wine

GLAZE INGREDIENTS:
1 egg white
powdered sugar
¼ cup fresh lemon juice

COOKIE FILLING INGREDIENTS:

2 pounds dried figs
1 pound shelled pecans
1 pound shelled almonds
1 small package chocolate chips
1 package raisins

1 pound package pitted dates
orange peeling, about 1 large orange
1 teaspoon cloves
1 teaspoon allspice
walnuts may be added

PROCEDURE:

To make dough, cream shortening and sugar. Add dry ingredients, then add enough wine to make a stiff dough, like bread dough. Knead until smooth. Roll out and cut in strips.

To make cookie filling, grind everything together except spices. Add about one pint fig preserves (mashed). If needed, add either water or orange juice, just enough to soften. Keep filling in refrigerator for further use.

Fill strips of dough with cookie filling. Bake at 350 degrees until lightly brown. Then top cookies for glaze.

Beat one egg white. Add powdered sugar and approximately ¼ cup of fresh lemon juice. This lemon glaze gives the fig cookies a tang.

Theresa Montalbano

ITALIAN FIG COOKIES

INGREDIENTS:

5 pounds all purpose flour
1 ½ pounds shortening
8 eggs
5 teaspoons vanilla
5 teaspoons baking powder
5 cups sugar
sprinkle of nutmeg and cinnamon
warm milk as needed

FILLING INGREDIENTS:

5 packages figs
1 package dates
1 large box raisins
1 package pecans
sprinkle of cinnamon
and black pepper
lemon and orange juice

PROCEDURE:

Ground figs, dates, raisins, and chop pecans coarsely. Mix pecans and ground fig mixture together. Sprinkle cinnamon and small amount of black pepper. Mix enough lemon and orange juice for spreading.

For dough, sift flour, baking powder and sugar in large pan. Mix shortening with flour until crumbly. Make a well. Combine eggs and vanilla. Pour into well. Mix thoroughly. Add warm milk as needed. Cover and let set about 4 hours. Take small piece of dough and roll out about 2 inches wide by 8 inches long. Put filling down middle. Bring each side over the other. Cut and bake at 375 degrees until lightly brown.

Johnny Ditcharo

ITALIAN FIG CAKES

INGREDIENTS:

FIG CAKES DOUGH

10 pounds flour	4 tablespoons vanilla
14 eggs (whole egg)	2 cans condensed milk
3½ cups lard	2¾ cups milk
4 cups sugar	3 sticks of butter (real butter)
4 tablespoons baking powder	a pinch of cinnamon in flour

FIG FILLING

4 pounds shelled pecans	1 pound dates
7 pounds figs, dried	5 8-ounce boxes raisins
4 tablespoons vanilla	3 oranges (use just rind)
4 cups sugar	3 tablespoons cinnamon
3 cups water	small amount syrup

PROCEDURE:

Warm milk, take off burner, mix sugar in milk real well, put in condensed milk, butter, lard, and vanilla and mix all these ingredients real well. Put flour in pan, sprinkle baking powder. Beat eggs real well, then make a well in flour by spreading flour away from center of pan. Add all of the milk and start working into flour by rubbing between your hands, mixing thoroughly. Knead dough and cut just enough dough to make about 4 fig cakes at a time. (when working on the cutting board, cover dough in pan with clean cloth, or piece of sheet). Roll out dough flat about 1 inch wide, fill with fig filling, roll so that filling is closed inside cake. Cut little slits into the side of the cake, about two will be enough. Place on ungreased cookie sheet about 2 inches apart and bake at about 425 to 450 degrees. Cakes will get light brown, but watch the bottom of cookies that they do not burn.

Take 3 cups water and sugar and cook down until it gets a little thick. After it's cool, pour into fig mixture (all ingredients for filling has to be ground with grinder, even orange rind). Mix all this together real well, put in small amount of syrup, just to soften fig mixture to work. NOTE: Grinding of fig filling ingredients may be done the night before you make the fig cakes.

Barbara Damico

FIG CAKES

INGREDIENTS FOR FILLING:

7 pounds dried figs
1 pound pitted dates
3 boxes raisins (7 ounce boxes)
1 pound fruit cake mix
2 orange peels (grated)

4 pounds pecans
3 ounces imitation vanilla
18 ounces light cane syrup
1 teaspoon cinnamon
3 cups sugar

INGREDIENTS FOR DOUGH:

1½ ounces imitation vanilla
1½ cups milk
2 cans condensed milk
4 cups sugar
3 blocks butter

4 cups shortening
16 eggs
10 pounds flour
9 teaspoons baking powder

PROCEDURE:

Grind the figs, dates, raisins, fruit cake mix and orange peels. Warm 1 cup water and melt sugar in it. Mix all ingredients together. To make dough, melt vanilla, milk, condensed milk, and sugar over low heat. Turn off heat. Add 3 blocks butter and shortening into warm mixture and mix well. Beat eggs well and mix into flour and baking powder. Then add the milk, condensed milk, sugar, vanilla, butter and shortening mixture by hand. Let dough stand for one hour before rolling.

Roll dough flat one inch wide. Place filling in center of dough. Roll dough closing filling inside dough. Cut in 2 inch sizes. Make two slits on top of cakes. Place on ungreased cookie sheet about one inch apart. Bake at 425 degrees until cakes are golden brown.

Rose Mascone

FIG CAKES

INGREDIENTS: (DOUGH)

5 pounds plain flour
1½ pounds shortening
6 tablespoons baking powder
3 cups sugar

3 cups water
8 eggs
2 tablespoons vanilla

INGREDIENTS: (FILLING)

3 pounds figs, finely ground
2 pounds candied fruit mix
1 pound raisins
1 cup pecans (Optional)

1 8-ounce jar cherries
1 cup water and sugar, dissolved
and worked in figs

PROCEDURE:

Mix dry ingredients for dough and shortening together until shortening is well blended. Add liquids for dough and beat eggs with a fork. Pour water a little at a time. You may not need all of the water. Roll out dough. Spread filling on dough.

To make filling, grind figs, candied fruit, raisins, cherries, and pecans together. dissolve sugar in water, and work in fig mixture. Spread on dough.

Santa Saladino

ANISE ITALIAN BISCOTTI

INGREDIENTS:

10 cups plain sifted flour
1½ tablespoons baking powder
1 cup sugar
1½ cups shortening

6 eggs (yolks only -- reserve
whites for icing)
1 teaspoon vanilla
milk (as much as needed)

INGREDIENTS FOR ICING:

3 boxes powdered sugar
⅓ cup of milk
6 egg whites

1 teaspoon anise oil
and/or anise extract

PROCEDURE:

In large mixing bowl, add flour, baking powder and sugar. Mix well. Add shortening and mix well; add egg yolks and vanilla. Add milk, mix well and knead until a fine consistency. Cut off a small piece of dough and roll into about 10-inch length, then cut into 2-inch lengths or shape into different sizes. Bake in 350 degree oven about 40 minutes. When cool, ice with anise icing, made as follows: Makes 24 dozen.

ANISE ICING

Beat egg whites until stiff; add powdered sugar gradually and anise oil and milk. Roll cookies in icing until well coated. Place on wax paper to dry.

Grace Panepinto

HAY STACKS OR PINULATI

INGREDIENTS:

5 pounds flour
1 pound shortening
5 teaspoons baking powder

1 teaspoon salt
1 dozen eggs

SYRUP INGREDIENTS:

2 cups cane syrup
2 cups sugar

PROCEDURE:

Sift flour, baking powder and salt. Mix shortening with flour until crumbly. Make a well and add eggs. Mix well. Take small piece and roll to resemble a pencil. Cut about one inch pieces. Fry in cooking oil in deep pot.

SYRUP:

Cook syrup and sugar together till small amount dropped in water forms a soft ball. Have small amount of cookies in pan and pour syrup over. Mix well. Turn out on table. Dip hands in cold water and shape cookies in hay stacks.

Johnnie Ditcharo

PINULATI

INGREDIENTS:

3 eggs	3 cups flour
1 teaspoon baking powder	3 tablespoons water
¼ teaspoon salt	½ cup honey

PROCEDURE:

Mix all ingredients except honey to make dough. With palms of hands roll pieces of dough to resemble a long pencil. Cut into ¼ inch pieces. Drop a few at a time into saucepan of hot lard. They will come to the top and pop like popcorn. When golden brown transfer with slotted ladle to absorbent paper. Put all into a large bowl, pour hot honey over all; stir quickly, with tablespoon. Scoop out a little at a time and shape into cluster on wax paper. One large serving.

Barbara Damico

ALMOND BISCOTTI

INGREDIENTS:

½ cup soft butter	3 cups sifted flour
1 cup sugar	3 teaspoons baking powder
1 teaspoon anise extract	1 teaspoon salt
3 eggs, beaten	1 cup finely chopped almonds

PROCEDURE:

Cream butter, sugar and anise extract until very light and fluffy. Beat in eggs until thoroughly blended. Resift flour with baking powder and salt. Add to creamed mixture. Stir in almonds. Turn out on lightly floured board and knead gently until smooth. Divide dough into 3 equal parts; form into rolls about 1½ inches in diameter. Place on lightly greased cookie sheet and bake at 350 degrees about 30 minutes or until rolls are firm to the touch. Remove from oven and let stand about 10 minutes. While still warm cut crosswise into slices ¾ inch thick. Lay slices cut side down on cookie sheets and return to oven at 350 degrees for 8 - 10 minutes or until light brown. Cool and store in airtight containers. Approximately 5 dozen.

Gene Elmer

AMMONIA COOKIES

INGREDIENTS:

5 pounds flour
3 cups sugar
1½ pounds shortening
5 level teaspoons ammonia powder

2 sticks butter
1 can milk
1 can water

ICING:

2 cups granulated sugar
2 cups water
5 drops anise oil

PROCEDURE:

Mix dry ingredients together. Work in shortening and butter. Add canned milk and water till dough is soft enough to make small balls. Place on cookie sheet about ½ inch apart. Bake till brown.

ICING:

Cook sugar, water and oil till you get a thin syrup. Put ⅓ cookies and ⅓ syrup in large pan. Mix until cookies are covered with glaze. Mix remaining cookies same way. Let sit till glaze turns white.

Helen Cannallato

SKIDELINA COOKIES

INGREDIENTS:

2 cups sugar or 1 pound
1 cup flour or ¼ pound
¼ teaspoon baking powder

1 orange rind
1 teaspoon cinnamon
1 teaspoon allspice

PROCEDURE:

Mix dry ingredients with a little water, about ¼ cup - making a hard dough. Add remaining ingredients. Roll dough into log shape, cut into 1½ inch pieces and flatten a little. Place pieces in pan on cloth and cover with another cloth. Let stand a ½ day or a day. Uncover them and bake 12 to 15 minutes at 350 degrees. Watch closely.

Genevieve Harris

CLOVE SUGAR COOKIES

INGREDIENTS:

5 pounds flour
8 eggs
1½ cups milk
1½ pound can lard
(use 1 pound can as your measure)

3 cups sugar
8 teaspoons baking powder
3½ heaping teaspoons cloves

PROCEDURE:

Put about 1 handful lard in milk and sugar, and heat -- do not boil. Sift flour in pan, sprinkle baking powder and cloves over flour. Add lard and mix lightly with finger tip; after thoroughly mixing, put in well beaten eggs and mix thoroughly. Pour in milk, sugar and lard that has been warmed, into a well of flour and add dry ingredients. Then start mixing all together by rubbing lightly. Knead a little then start cutting into strips about 2 or 3 inches long. Roll this strip out on large table or board, unfloured. Cut rolled dough, (leave dough rolled do not flatten out) into 2 inch pieces. Pinch each piece by holding it in between your thumb and forefinger. Place cookies on ungreased cookie sheet about 2 inches apart and bake in a 475 or 500 degree oven about 5 to 10 minutes. Cookies will not be very brown on top but look at the bottom.

ICING FOR SUGAR COOKIES:

3¾ boxes of powdered sugar
1 stick of butter to 1 box of sugar
1 to 2 tablespoons pet milk or to a spreadable texture.

Barbara Damico

ITALIAN SPICE COOKIES

INGREDIENTS:

7 cups sifted all purpose flour
2 cups sugar
1 cup cocoa
7 teaspoons baking powder
1 teaspoon cinnamon

1 teaspoon cloves (ground)
1 cup shortening
2 eggs
1½ cups milk

ICING INGREDIENTS:

1 box powdered sugar
milk (as much as needed)

PROCEDURE:

Sift dry ingredients in a large bowl. Add shortening, eggs, and milk. Mix well. Drop by teaspoon on a lightly greased cookie sheet. Bake at 375 degrees for about 25 - 30 minutes. Makes about 10 dozen.

To make icing, add milk to powdered sugar and mix until the thickness of cream. Drop cookies into icing and stir until cookies are well coated or glazed. Makes 10 dozen.

Grace Panepinto

ITALIAN DOUGH BALLS

INGREDIENTS:

2 eggs
1 cup sugar
1½ teaspoons vanilla

1 cup milk
4 cups flour
2 heaping tablespoons baking powder

PROCEDURE:

Mix eggs, sugar and vanilla together. Pour into milk and mix well. Make a well in the flour, sprinkle in baking powder and then pour in wet ingredients. Mix well until smooth. Put about 4 inches of oil in a 2 quart pot and let it get real hot on a medium fire. Take about a teaspoon of batter and drop into hot grease, let fry until golden brown. (Make sure grease is hot, but not too hot to cook dough too fast for they will burn on the outside and not cook on the inside). Makes 1 to 2 dozen.

Barbara Damico

SEED COOKIES

INGREDIENTS:

8 cups plain flour
2 cups sugar
1 pound shortening
1 teaspoon soda

1 tablespoon vanilla
4 eggs
½ cup scalded milk
sesame seeds

PROCEDURE:

Mix ingredients, add shortening, vanilla, eggs and milk -- mix well. Roll into log shape and over seeds. Cut into 3 inch or 4 inch logs. Place in oven at 350 degrees until golden brown. Rinse seeds in colander and drain until ready to use.

Lillian Saladino

PECAN COOKIES

INGREDIENTS:

5 pounds plain flour	1 pound shortening
7 whole eggs, well beaten	1 large can evaporated milk
6 tablespoons baking powder	¼ cup homogenized milk
2 heaping teaspoons cinnamon	1 one-ounce bottle pure almond extract
3 cups sugar	3 cups chopped pecans
2 blocks butter	

PROCEDURE:

Mix flour, baking powder, cinnamon and pecans in large pan. Mix sugar, shortening and butter in separate large container until well blended. Then add evaporated milk, homogenized milk, almond extract and well beaten eggs. Mix well. Add all ingredients together. Take small pieces of dough and roll on board about ½ inch around. Cut in one inch pieces or as desired. Bake at 350 or 375 degrees until very light brown.

Rose Mascone

LEMON PECAN RINGS

INGREDIENTS:

2 cups sifted flour	1 cup pecans ground
½ teaspoon baking soda	1 teaspoon cinnamon
½ teaspoon salt	1 egg
½ cup corn oil	1 tablespoon grated lemon rind
½ cup granulated sugar	3 tablespoons lemon juice
½ cup brown sugar, firmly packed	1 cup Bran flakes

PROCEDURE:

Blend together sugars, oil, egg and lemon juice. In another bowl mix together flour, soda, salt, cinnamon, lemon rind, flakes and pecans.

Add liquid to dry ingredients and mix well. Drop by teaspoons full, about size of walnut, two inches apart on well greased baking sheet. Dip spoon in lemon juice. Flatten out and make hole in the center of each using back of teaspoon.

Bake in moderate oven 350 degrees about 15 minutes or until lightly browned. Remove from baking sheet at once, cool or wire rack or plate. Makes about 3½ dozen cookies.

Lorraine Taravella

LEMON BARS

INGREDIENTS:

1 cup butter
¼ teaspoon salt
½ cup powdered sugar
2 cups flour
4 eggs, slightly beaten
4 tablespoons lemon juice
2 cups sugar
4 tablespoons flour
grated rind of 1 lemon
2 tablespoons sifted powdered sugar for dusting

PROCEDURE:

Blend first four ingredients well and press into a greased 10 by 13 inch baking dish. bake at 350 degrees for 20-30 minutes. Mix remaining five ingredients together and pour over first mixture. Bake 20-30 minutes at 325 degrees or until firm. Dust with sifted powdered sugar and cut when cool. Keep in refrigerator. Makes 5 dozen.

Gene Elmer

Puddings

CRACKER PUDDING

INGREDIENTS:

1 - ½ large can of evaporated cream
5 eggs, separated

2 teaspoons vanilla
1 ⅔ cups sugar
10 soda crackers

PROCEDURE:

Beat egg whites and set aside. In a quart and a half casserole, mix egg yolks and sugar. Add cream and mix well. Soak crackers in water. Squeeze water out and mix wet crackers in above mixture. Add vanilla. Fold in egg whites, stiffly beaten. Set casserole bowl into larger baking bowl fitted with a little water. Bake at 375 degrees for one hour and 15 minutes, or until knife inserted comes out clean. Serves 6.

Johnnie Ditcharo

MIRLITON PUDDING

INGREDIENTS:

6 mirlitons
⅓ cup flour
1 stick of soft butter
4 eggs
1 cup pecans
1 cup raisins
¼ cup chopped cherries

½ cup grated coconut
2 teaspoons vanilla
2 teaspoons ground nutmeg
½ cup evaporated milk
⅓ to ½ cup sugar (to taste)
nutmeg

PROCEDURE:

Boil mirlitons an hour or until tender enough to be scraped from shell. Remove from water and cool enough to handle. Cut in half lengthwise, remove large seed from center and scrape out pulp. Pre-heat oven 275 degrees.

In a large bowl cream mirlitons, butter, eggs, vanilla and milk. Gradually stir in sugar, flour and nutmeg. Mix well. Fold in pecans, cherries, raisins and coconut. Pour into buttered 12 x 9 x 2 inch baking pan. Sprinkle with nutmeg. Bake one hour and 15 minutes or until knife inserted halfway between center and edge comes out clean. Serve pudding warm or cool. Serving for 8 or 10.

Mrs. Rose Mascone

VANILLA BREAD PUDDING AND SAUCE

INGREDIENTS:

6 tablespoons sugar	**1/8 teaspoon salt**
2 tablespoons flour	**2 teaspoons butter**

PROCEDURE:

Stir ¾ cup boiling water, add all ingredients, boil 2 minutes, stirring. Remove from heat and add ½ cup milk and 2 teaspoons vanilla.

BREAD PUDDING

2¼ cups bread	**¼ teaspoon salt**
2 eggs	**2¼ cups milk**
½ cup sugar	**½ teaspoon vanilla**
	2 tablespoons butter

Scald milk and add all ingredients, pour over bread. Beat egg whites with sugar and fold into mixture. Bake in 350 degree oven for about 40 minutes. Top with the vanilla pudding sauce.

Genevieve Panepinto Harris

COLD ZABAGLIONE

INGREDIENTS:

6 eggs	**1/8 teaspoon cinnamon**
⅔ cups sugar	**¼ teaspoon vanilla**
¾ cup sweet Marsala	**¾ cup heavy cream, whipped**
grated rind of ½ lemon	

PROCEDURE:

Beat the egg yolks only with sugar in bowl or top of a double boiler until the yolks are light and frothy. Add Marsala, lemon rind, cinnamon and vanilla. Place bowl or top of double boiler over hot water, beating the eggs constantly. Do not allow water to boil. As soon as the Zabaglione swells up and is light and even in texture, remove it from the heat and continue stirring until cool. Gently add the whipped cream. Chill and serve in individual dishes accompanied by cookies. Place a garnish of whipped cream on each serving. Serves 4.

Colette Bosco

Fried Pastry

PANE

INGREDIENTS:

10 cups flour
2 small packages compressed or
2 small packages dried yeast

2 cups lukewarm water
2 eggs
2 teaspoons salt

PROCEDURE:

Sift flour into large bowl or onto large board. Make well in middle of flour, add yeast which has been dissolved in ½ cup lukewarm water. Add salt, eggs, remaining water, and mix well. Knead dough well for about 10 to 15 minutes until smooth and elastic. Place in a greased bowl. Turn dough over, and cover with wax paper and towel. Let rise ina a warm place until double in bulk (about 2 hours). Divide dough in two. Roll each piece into an oblong shape and roll, working the dough until each loaf is about 1 foot long. Place on greased cookie sheet. Brush top with a mixture of beaten egg yolk and little water. Make a few slashes on top of each loaf with knife. Let rise until double in bulk. Bake in a 425 degree oven for 10 minutes. Reduce heat to 375 degrees and continue baking for 25 minutes. Cool on rack. Makes two loaves.

Grace Panepinto

BANANA BREAD

INGREDIENTS:

3 - 4 bananas
1 stick melted oleo or butter
1 cup sugar
2 eggs, beaten
1 teaspoon baking soda

¼ cup coconut
¼ cup pecan pieces
1½ cups plain flour
cinnamon and nutmeg to taste

PROCEDURE:

Mash ripe bananas. Mix with bananas, oleo, sugar, eggs, baking soda, coconut, pecan pieces, cinnamon and nutmeg. Blend in flour. Pour in greased pan. Bake 40-45 minutes at 350 degrees.

Theresa Lucia Frickey

EGGPLANT FRITTERS

INGREDIENTS:

4 cups self-rising flour
1½ cups brown sugar, packed
3 teaspoons cinnamon
1 teaspoon allspice
2 tablespoons vanilla flavoring
1 beaten egg with enough milk to make 1 cup liquid
1 eggplant, cooked and mashed (about 1½ to 2 cups)

PROCEDURE:

Mix all ingredients with electric mixer for 1 minute. Deep fry, dropping by teaspoonful into medium hot Crisco. Drain on paper towel. Batter does not have to be cooked at one time. It will keep several days stored in air-tight bowl in refrigerator.

OPTIONAL
Coat with granulated sugar, confectioner's sugar, or cinnamon and sugar while still warm.

Anna Mae Saluto St. Pierre

SPINGE

INGREDIENTS:

4 eggs
¼ cup melted margarine
2½ cups flour

2 envelopes dried yeast
1 cup warm water
1 teaspoon salt
1 teaspoon vanilla

PROCEDURE:

Dissolve yeast in warm water. Beat eggs, add yeast and melted shortening. Add flour and salt and vanilla. Beat thoroughly. Let rise until double in bulk. Beat again for one minute. Let rise again. Dough should be quite soft. If too runny, add a little more flour. Drop by spoonsful into hot oil. Fry until golden brown. Will rise to surface like sponges (hence name in Italian). Drain and cool. Pour honey over them and sprinkle with finely chopped almonds or walnuts.

Mae Bingo

CASATELLI

INGREDIENTS:

6 eggs, well beaten	**cottage cheese**
3 tablespoons sugar	**honey**
½ cup vegetable oil	**powdered sugar**
flour	

FILLING:

1 pound ricotta or cottage cheese	**1 teaspoon cinnamon**
sugar to taste, about ½ cup	

PROCEDURE:

To eggs add sugar and vegetable oil. Add enough flour to this mixture to handle like pie crust dough. Roll out to about 1/8 inch thickness. Fill with cottage cheese filling. Seal well (make crescent shapes) about size of 4 inch glass rim. You may seal with milk and press with fork. Fry in deep fat oil until light brown. Drain well on paper towels. Sprinkle with honey and powdered sugar.

FILLING:

About one pound ricotta or cottage cheese, add sugar to taste (about ½ cup). Add about 1 teaspoon cinnamon (again to taste). Fill dough as above.

Mae Bingo

FRIED PASTRY

INGREDIENTS:

3 cups sifted flour	**4 egg yolks, slightly beaten**
pinch of salt	**1 tablespoon rum, brandy or**
2 tablespoons confectioners sugar	**any white wine**
2 eggs, slightly beaten	**2 cups peanut or salad oil**

PROCEDURE:

Sift flour and salt with sugar and resift. Make a well in center of dry ingredients, and put eggs, egg yolks and rum into it. Knead thoroughly for 10 minutes until smooth. Add more flour if dough is too soft. This should be firm dough. Cover dough with towel and let stand one hour. Divide dough into 4 parts. Roll one part at a time out on a light floured board to paper thinness. Cut into strips ½ inch wide and 6 inches long. Tie each strip into a loose bow knot or twist. Place on cloth and let dry for 5 minutes. Fry bowknot in hot 375 degree oil until lightly browned, turning once. Lift out of oil carefully with slotted spoon and drain on unglazed paper. Place drained bowknot on large plate and sprinkle with powdered sugar. Serves 8 - 10.

Grace Panepinto

Pies

CARAMEL PIE

INGREDIENTS:

1 can of condensed milk boiled for 8 hours in a pot. Be sure can is covered with water at all times. Refrigerate over nite.

1 pie crust made from graham crackers or vanilla wafers.

PROCEDURE:

Slice bananas very thin to cover bottom of pie shell then a layer of caramel (condensed milk) continue with layers until all caramel is used. Cover top of pie with coolwhip and serve immediately.

PECAN HALVES

Use large pecan halves, dip in slightly beaten egg white, then roll in granulated sugar to which cinnamon has been added, and bake.

MYSTERY PIE

INGREDIENTS:

3 egg whites
1 cup sugar
½ to 1 cup pecans, chopped

1 teaspoon vanilla
23 Ritz crackers crushed
instant hot cocoa mix

PROCEDURE:

Beat egg whites, adding sugar gradually. When stiff, fold in crushed Ritz crackers, pecans, and vanilla. Pour into greased pie pan and bake for 30 minutes. Cool. Top with whipped cream with 1 tablespoon cocoa mix whipped into it. Sprinkle more cocoa mix over top and refrigerate for one hour.

Esther Stringer

ITALIAN ANISETTE PIE

INGREDIENTS:

1 cup graham cracker crumbs
2 tablespoons melted butter
3 envelopes unflavored gelatin
⅓ cup sugar
3 tablespoons instant coffee
1½ cups tap water

4-jiggers (ounces) anisette
1½ cups evaporated milk
1 large carton of whipped cream topping
orange sections peeled or drained
peach slices

PROCEDURE:

Mix crumbs and butter; butter a 9 inch pie plate and press mixture into the bottom and sides of pie plate evenly -- set aside. Mix gelatin and sugar in saucepan; make instant coffee using tap water, coffee and anisette. Add to gelatin mix and stir over low heat until gelatin is dissolved and mixture is lukewarm. Stir in milk and chill until fairly firm, stirring occasionally. Fold in 1 cup of whipped cream topping and refrigerate until real firm. Just before serving, decorate with remaining whipped cream topping and fruit.

SODA CRACKER PIE

INGREDIENTS:

3 egg whites
¼ teaspoon cream of tartar
1 cup sugar
16 saltine crackers (crushed & rolled)

1 cup chopped nuts
1 teaspoon vanilla
cool whip topping

PROCEDURE:

Beat egg whites until fluffy. Add cream of tartar, beat until real stiff. Gradually add sugar. Fold in crackers, nuts and vanilla. Mix together and bake in ungreased pie plate at 350 degrees for thirty minutes. Cool completely. Place cool whip on pie. Set in ice box for two hours. (Optional - Sprinkle top with angle flake coconut.)

Voris King

Candy

FUDGE

INGREDIENTS:

2 cans condensed milk
4½ cups sugar
1 block butter

4 tablespoons marshmallow cream
pecans or 8-ounce peanut butter
½ cup cocoa

PROCEDURE:

Mix cocoa and a little water to make paste. Add paste, sugar, condensed milk in pot and mix well. Stir fudge at all times. When it starts to boil, test it in water until you see that it forms a soft ball. When the fudge is ready, take pot off fire and add butter. Add pecans or peanut butter and marshmallow cream. Continue to stir till all is mixed well. Pour in buttered dish. Cut fudge after it has hardened.

Anna Mae Rotolo

CHOCOLATE PECAN FUDGE

INGREDIENTS:

4 cups sugar
1 package chocolate pudding
2 level teaspoons cocoa
1 can large evaporated milk

¾ block butter
1 tablespoon vanilla
1 7-ounce jar marshmallow creme
1 pound chopped pecans or 2½ cups

PROCEDURE:

Combine first four ingredients and cook over medium heat until a small amount of mixture forms a ball when dropped in cold water when pressed together. This takes about 30 minutes. Remove from stove, add butter and beat well. Beat in vanilla and marshmallow creme until it begins to harden some. Then add pecans and mix well. Beat again until almost hard. Pour in buttered platter. After it cools, cut in pieces.

Lorraine Taravella

FUDGE

INGREDIENTS:

4 cups sugar
1 pack chocolate pudding
1/8 teaspoon salt
2 tablespoons cocoa
1 tall can evaporated milk

1 tablespoon white corn syrup
½ block butter
1 tablespoon vanilla
1 8-ounce jar marshmallow creme
2 cups chopped pecans or walnuts

PROCEDURE:

Grease a heavy gauge saucepan well with butter. Sift together sugar, pudding, salt and cocoa into pot. Add milk, syrup, and butter. Mix well and put on medium heat. Cook until a soft ball forms or 242 degrees on a candy thermometer, stirring occasionally. Remove from heat and add vanilla, marshmallow creme, and nuts. Beat about 5 minutes by hand until gloss is gone. Pour into a buttered 9 x 13 inch pan. When cool to the touch, just score into size you want. When cold, finish cutting.

Nancy Randazzo

HEAVENLY HASH CANDY

INGREDIENTS:

2 6-ounce packs semi-sweet chocolate chips*
1 cup crunchy peanut butter
4 cups miniature marshmallows

*You can substitute 1 6-ounce semi-sweet and 1 6-ounce milk chocolate chips.

PROCEDURE:

Melt chocolate chips and peanut butter in a heavy saucepan. Remove from heat occasionally so as not to overheat chocolate mixture. Stir continually. When melted, remove completely from heat and fold in marshmallows lightly, to coat with chocolate and not to crush marshmallows. Pour into greased 9 x 9 inch pan and chill. Cut just before serving.

If you have plastic egg molds, butter the top and bottom of egg molds. Fill both with mixture and close tightly. Chill until firm. Remove from mold by using the point of a knife just around the edge of the mold where it was put together and egg will come out neatly. Wrap with plastic food wrap or aluminum foil or if you want to decorate with icing to be nice and fancy.

Nancy Randazzo

NETTA'S PRALINES

INGREDIENTS:

2 cups light brown sugar
2 cups white sugar
1 cup pet cream

2 cups whole pecans
4 tablespoons butter
2 teaspoons vanilla

PROCEDURE:

Cook sugar and cream until it comes to a boil. Cook 10 to 15 minutes and test until it forms a soft ball in cold water. Take off fire and add butter, vanilla and pecans. Drop by spoonfuls on aluminum foil.

Netta Thomassie

BOURBON BALLS

INGREDIENTS:

2¼ cups vanilla wafer fine crumbs
1 cup finely chopped pecans
2/3 cup bourbon

1 cup confectioners sugar
3 tablespoons cocoa
2 tablespoons white corn syrup

PROCEDURE:

Break vanilla wafers into small pieces. Add a few pieces into blender at a time. Blend to crumbs. Put into bowl, add pecans. Mix well. Place remaining ingredients into container. Blend for about 10 seconds. Pour blend over dry ingredients and mix well. Roll into balls one inch in diameter, then roll balls in more confectioners sugar. Store in airtight container. Age from 18 to 24 hours before serving. Makes 40 to 48 balls.

Lena R. Ales

Beverages

THE WINES OF ITALY

Italy is full of wines. Italy boasts a wide range of climates and soils, and therefore a huge variety of wines. The Grape varieties are distinctly Italian. Most of Italy is mountainous, and most of the grapes which produce Italian wines are hill grown. Italian wines travel very well and provide an excellent accompaniment to any cuisine.

There are many different regions in Italy, and they produce different types of wines. Not all Italian wines are known in the United States. The most popular according to sales is Lambrusco, which comes from the region of Emilia Romagna. Lambrusco, a unique, dry, semi-sparkling red, comes from the grape of the same name. Fragrant, fresh and clean, its red froth quickly subsides leaving a pronounced prickle.

The second most popular is the wines of the Veneto region — Valpolicella, Bardolino, and Soave. *Valpolicella* is a cherry red wine with a gentle sweet smell and a nice trace of bitterness in the aftertaste. *Bardolino,* from the same grapes grown in the lighter soils, is a lighter red with a refreshing touch of sharpness. *Soave,* perhaps Italy's most famous white wine, is a dry, pale, very well balanced wine with a hint of floweriness.

The other wines that are becoming known are Barolo, Barbaresco, and Barbera from the Piedmont region. Also from the Piedmont region comes a white, sparkling, semi-sweet wine called Asti Spumante. From the Tuscany region comes Chianti, perhaps the most famous name from Italy; a red wine that can vary from light to heavy. Listed are a few names of Italian wines which you may recognize.

Region . . . . Lombardy
Wines. . . . . Inferno, Grumello, Sassella
Region . . . . Marches
Wines. . . . . Verdicchio

One of the newest, fastest growing wines from Italy is the Corvo red and white from Sicily. Corvo red is a fine, velvety wine with an interesting aroma. The Corvo white is fresh, attractive and full with the right degree of acidity.

The wines of Italy are some of the best values today. The wines are good quality and most prices are below $5.00 per bottle.

S A L U T E

Joseph Miceli, President
American Italian Federation of Louisiana

PONCE DI VINO
(Punch)

INGREDIENTS:

Fifth Italian red wine: claret or burgundy	rind of lemon
1/2 inch pieces stick cinnamon OR	rind of one orange
1/4 teaspoon ground cloves	1/2 cup sugar

PROCEDURE:

Pour wine in stainless steel or enamel pan and add cinnamon stick, lemon rind, orange rind, and sugar. Bring to a boil for one minute. Remove from stove and serve immediately in cup or mugs.

Grace Panepinto

CHAMPAGNE PUNCH

INGREDIENTS:

5 ounces orange curacao	1 pint lemon juice
2 pints cognac	5 ounces Maraschino syrup
1/2 pint rum	1 pint pineapple juice
1 cup sugar	4 bottles pink champagne

PROCEDURE:

Mix all ingredients except champagne. When ready to serve, pour mixed ingredients into large punch bowl over block of ice. Add champagne and stir. Serves 30 champagne glasses.

Chris Arnold

INDEX

ANTIPASTO

SOUPS

PASTA, SAUCES and CHEESE

VEGETABLES and CASSEROLES

SEAFOOD

POULTRY

MEATS

SALADS

CAKES

COOKIES

PUDDINGS

FRIED PASTRY

PIES

CANDY

BEVERAGES